BEYOND THE OBVIOUS

Dr CHRISTINE PAGE
MBBS, MRCGP, DCH, DRCOG, MFHom

Beyond
the Obvious

BRINGING INTUITION INTO
OUR AWAKENING CONSCIOUSNESS

INDEX COMPILED BY MARK KIRKNESS

SAFFRON WALDEN
THE C.W. DANIEL COMPANY LIMITED

First published in Great Britain in 1998
by The C.W. Daniel Company Limited
1 Church Path, Saffron Walden,
Essex, CB10 1JP, United Kingdom

ISBN 9780852073223

Produced in association with Book Production Consultants plc,
25–27 High Street, Chesterton, Cambridge CB4 1ND,
Typeset by Ward Partnership, Saffron Walden, Essex
Printed and bound by CPI Antony Rowe, Chippenham, Wiltshire

Contents

Dedication

*To the heart of Mankind and to those who
guide and support us at this precious time*

Acknowledgement

*To Pat Jarvis for her proof reading
and loving guidance*

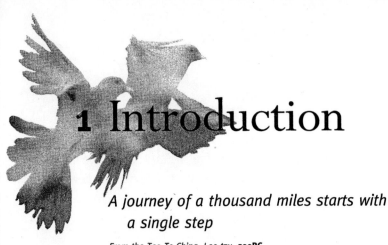

1 Introduction

*A journey of a thousand miles starts with
    a single step*

From the Tao Te Ching, Lao-tzu, **500BC**

This is a story concerning an extraordinary journey, a journey of initiation. It happens to embody many of my own experiences, but it is not unique to me. By changing the characters, scenery and dialogue, you may find that I am actually recounting aspects of *your* own life which are deeply personal and often concealed even from those whom you consider to be intimate friends.

The journey takes us into the very essence of our being where nothing is hidden, where man-made boundaries are unnecessary and where we are immersed within the creative force of all life. Our guide on the path is *intuition*. Our goal is to incorporate that intuition into our awakening consciousness. This ageless friend entices us to discover what, on some level, we have always known; it is the oroborus, the snake which eats its own tail, and where the end becomes the beginning. The human concept of order tends to describe such a journey in linear terms and yet in essence we have already arrived.

Intuition is the compassionate observer. It is the wise part of ourselves which formulates a resolve based on its ability to assimilate all the information available from the various functions of the mind which include the psychic senses, logic, emotions and instincts. It is non-judgemental, recognising the value, at some level, of all things and yet can discern which path would bring greatest benefit to all concerned.

It has therefore been described as *'intellect without fear'* and as *'the synthesis of our instincts, emotions and logic'*. The awareness it brings is not just frivolous fancy but relies on a firm foundation of experience and understanding as well as the ability to express and release our emotions appropriately. Hence it is important that we become fully conversant with our thoughts and feelings so that they can work in harmony with the intuition and not against it.

As the channel within our mind becomes clearer, the intuition appears to surface from nowhere and fails to observe a logical sequence of deduction and yet it evokes the tell-tale: *'Ah-ha!'*. This *'inner knowing as it essentially exists'* carries with it such a sense of certainty that, when we trust and follow it, nobody can dissuade us from our path (quotes from Alice Bailey; see Bibliography).

This self-assurance is the result of a transformation of consciousness which carries the pilgrim from the dormant state of *not caring*, through the emotional phase of *hoping*, via the logical step of *believing* until the ultimate goal of *knowing* is reached, reflecting pure inner guidance.

Intuition is not exclusive to the spiritually elite but is readily available to every individual and can be compared to radio signals travelling the airways waiting for us to tune into their particular frequency. It is often referred to as a *gut feeling* or *sixth sense* although men usually prefer to call it a *hunch* which they have learnt from past performance is a reliable source of trustworthy advice.

Intuition is present in the very air we breathe, within our deepest thoughts, during moments of creative dreaming and is the enigmatic friend whose flash of insight steers us away from danger and towards people or situations, which we then call synchronicity.

As a medical student of the seventies, I was taught that 80% of my diagnosis should come from the patient's history, 15% from examination and only 5% from tests. How times have changed! In subjects such as neurology, we were expected to reach a diagnosis before the patient sat down by observing their mode of walking, their posture and any other useful, often subtle, clues. In such a highly scientific training, my professors would never have said: *'We want to improve your intuitive skills'*, but that's what happened.

By the time I reached general practice, I was dependent on my sixth sense to recognise the seriously sick patient whose history was vague and non-specific, especially when seeing over 40 patients per day. I remember being taught *'listen to the mother; she knows when her child is ill even though there are few outward signs'*. This wise advice helped me to recognise more than one childhood cancer at an early stage when treatment was highly successful.

I defy any doctor or other health care professional to deny their reliance on intuition for enhancing their clinical acumen, although I am fairly sure they would say: *'You just know these things'* which usually suggests a large degree of experience mixed with the all-important pinch of inner knowing.

As we journey towards an intimate relationship with our intuition, it is not uncommon to distrust its messages believing that they will appear illogical to others, be the source of ridicule or rejection, separate us from those we love, mimic mild insanity or lead to pain and failure. These concerns are not unreasonable and indeed may surface along the journey and yet, when we look beyond these fears, we recognise the profound gifts that this *still small voice* offers:

- Enrichment of life experiences
- The opportunity to look beyond the obvious
- Clarity in decision-making
- Greater ability to connect with others on a soul level
- Increasing insights into the Greater Plan
- The knowledge that we are contributing to this Plan
- Accelerated soul growth and fulfilment
- The ability to be in the right place at the right time
- The chance to know ourselves and hence to know our Creator

As you can see, development of the intuition is not concerned purely with enhancing personal prowess, increasing psychic abilities, being able to *'read other people'* in order to stay in control or expanding creative skills so as to achieve success in business. These are bonuses which are gained along the way but we limit our full potential when we consider them to be the goals on this sacred journey.

Intuition possesses the feminine qualities of connection linking us, in varying degrees, to:

- The core of our Being; our soul
- The soul of every person upon this Earth
- All other life forms usually through a group soul
- The world of Spirit
- The Creator, God, the Universal Life Force, or the Eternal Light

This inner knowing is channelled mainly through two of the energy centres, or *chakras*, within spiritual man; the first being the place of soul resonance, the Heart, and the second, the seat of wisdom within the mind, the Third Eye.

 ## Meditation

One of the main keys to developing a steady state of intuition is through the practice of meditation which facilitates the ability to calm the mind from the normal state of *hyperchatter* and allow it to become settled in the moment. Techniques such as using a mantra or an image, concentrating on the breath or creating a vacuum within the mental arena, all aid the experience and have been used for thousands of years by those who recognise the demanding nature of our highly developed intellect.

Although allowing the body to come to rest assists the creation of a sacred space, it is well established that a meditative state can also be successfully induced through rhythmic, physical movement such as walking and dancing, as seen in the *whirling dervishes*.

Meditation grants us the time and space to be still. Here we may receive guidance through images or words or find ourselves within a place where we can resonate with the tone and frequency of our pure spirit. The mind and body rejoice when they are given the opportunity to dance to this eternal music, allowing them to reject all other notes which are disharmonic to the soul.

Looking back over my life, I can recognise the various stages of development of my own inner knowing and although still a traveller, can see the tremendous changes which have occurred over the decades especially when I remember emerging into the brilliant sunlight from what appeared to be a dense fog, which for years had caused me to feel confused, disorientated and helpless.

I doubt whether there is an end point to this journey for each apparent completion takes us to a higher or deeper dimension in the spiral of life through continual cycles of order and chaos, build-up and breakdown, in-breath and expiration. On this earthly plane we see this succession of creativity readily reflected, with much of nature recognising the need to allow some part of itself to die before the next level of growth can appear.

Even in the darkest moments of our life or when we are deeply entrenched within the world of matter the inner urgings of the intuition persist, sending out their signals and providing a lifeline to the soul who takes the time to stop and move its focus from dense gravitational images.

As the eternal light penetrates the shadows, we become aware of an engaging serpentine path which makes its way through a variety of challenges and opportunities all of which entice us to hone our skill of inner knowing until it becomes *a state of being* rather than just *another function of the mind*.

This is a shamanistic pilgrimage where the individual experiences themselves in all their glory, facing their fears and their joys, and moves through the worlds of ignorance, limitation, illusion, glamour and pride.

There are many *sirens* on the path attracting us towards different horizons and yet they are in themselves a gift, strengthening our inner resolve to stay on track. In reality there is no time and therefore even though we are held by their haunting song for months or sometimes years, it is the decision to return to our path which is so soul enhancing.

The journey towards integration of intuition consists of seven stages:

1 **The Awakening:** Stepping Out

2 **Expansion:** Taking on One's Own Power

3 **Thought liberation:** Clearing a Path through the Mind

4 **Harnessing the will:** The Power to Direct Energy

5 **Taking a stand:** Making Decisions from One's Inner Truth

6 **Letting go of the result:** Detached Compassion

7 **True connection:** Merging the Ego with the Soul

We rarely meet these stages in isolation from each other and may find that we have completed stage 5 in our work environment only to be struggling with stage 1 in our relationships. At other times we may not even notice passing from one phase to the next as it was so effortless.

There will be many *awakenings* throughout life as we come to accept and integrate those parts of ourselves still in the shadows. The journey is not a competition but rather an initiation process which provides us with infinite opportunities to learn, grow and enjoy life whilst being able to contribute to the Universal consciousness. Although the goal is to function from our inner knowing, it is our willingness to take part which is more important than completion of the course.

As I describe the various phases, I shall offer insights from my own life which will hopefully clarify the message as well as act as a mirror for your own life's experiences. So before we progress further, let me tell you more about myself.

During a recent visit to my mother, I was shown an old family photograph album which was crammed full of sepia pictures of my ancestors posing for the camera in the manner of the times. Amongst the photos was one of my mother's grandmother who, with her hair tied neatly back and wearing a velvet dress with a high neck and puff sleeves, could have been any age. She looks out into the distance and for a while I become lost in her thoughts and dreams.

For someone who lived long before the Great Wars in the picturesque border lands of Scotland, I wonder what she would make of the hustle and bustle of this highly technological age. As I study her face, I suspect that she would have rolled up her sleeves and attended to the practical needs of the moment whilst imparting words of wisdom, which are probably as relevant to the people of today as they were then.

She was a woman ahead of her time as was her daughter, my grandmother (whom I never knew on this physical plane), and my own mother. My mother recalls that during holidays spent with her grandmother, the latter was often called by the vicar or the doctor to attend someone who needed help. Archetypically, she was the wise woman of the neighbourhood with an eclectic job description which required her to move from midwife to counsellor, to social worker and even to being the one who laid out the dead. She was nobody's fool and believed in speaking her truth although this was always delivered with compassion and generosity of heart.

In her work she encompassed the inherent female ability to appreciate the mystical process of birth and death, daring to enter the interdimensional space where the will of the individual merges with the will of the Source. Earlier in history, women who attended births and deaths were considered to have supernatural powers and many were persecuted and lost their lives because they chose not to abandon those who needed them at this time of transition.

Thankfully, by the time my great-grandmother was born, in the middle of the 19th Century, thinking had changed and she was allowed to pursue her work undisturbed. When she retired the town honoured the service she had given by presenting her with a walking stick topped by a silver lion's head.

It seemed natural for my grandmother to carry on these traditions. The family had by then moved to the outskirts of Edinburgh and it was common practice for my mother's childhood home to be open-house to all those who required sound advice, encouragement or the warm hospitality which was being offered, especially at hogmanay! As with her mother, her common sense and opinions were sought by many and it was not unusual to find the *laird* of the manor, the minister of the church or a neighbour sitting at the kitchen table discussing the matters of the day.

I feel honoured to have inherited these precious gifts from my mother's lineage and recognise them to include wisdom, integrity, honesty, curiosity, compassion and generosity. It is easy to see these same qualities in my own mother who has lived her life with an unshakeable yet uncomplicated faith, a generosity of spirit and as a constant seeker after the truth.

Each of these women had the ability to look beyond the obvious, to know things which had not yet taken place on the physical plane, to be compassionate though objective and to offer help beyond their own personal needs. As this book will reveal, these are requisite ingredients for working with the intuition where we merge our consciousness with that of another whilst keeping our feet firmly on the ground and our heart connected to the eternal Source.

So as not to perpetuate the myth that intuition is mainly a female prerogative, let me add that my father possessed complementary qualities which helped me to navigate the waters of life. He was sensitive, compassionate, totally committed to his work and family, diplomatic and, most important of all for a young child, great fun. He told the most awful jokes which were usually met with groans and still continued undeterred. He saw life as an adventure and would be the first to climb a mountain, enter unknown waters or attempt to speak a foreign language when travelling abroad. However, he never expected the same initiatives from other people, delighted if he met a fellow pioneer but always content to go it alone.

His relatively sudden death when I was 17 years old, turned my life around and yet I never felt anything but extremely privileged that he had imparted to me his inspiration, encouragement and love during the most formative years of my life.

Death was never a fear for me and we used to joke that by my mid-twenties, I had more family on the *other side* than I did on this side.

My father's passing was helped by the fact that my mother had a rich understanding of the fourth dimensional or psychic world and I personally received valuable evidence of the afterlife which was irrefutable in my mind.

I have always been very fortunate to receive spiritual guidance from my father, my grandmothers and others who have passed from my soul family. My father makes his presence known through a soft touch on my lower back and then I hear his thoughts in my mind. I can remember it suddenly dawning on me that, at a time when most teenagers would rather their parents were not present, here was my father who was undeterred by closed doors!

Despite this revelation, in all our time together I have received only tremendous love and an acknowledgement that I am totally free to live my life to my own design and that he has no expectations or hidden agenda. I've experienced this same detached compassion from those in the spirit world during the 20 plus years of my work in the caring professions as a doctor, homoeopath and teacher.

I recall that on many occasions whilst listening to someone who believes they are totally unlovable and beyond forgiveness, seeing them surrounded by radiant colours of love streaming forth from those who care for them on the other side. Our spirit family's unfailing love, despite any feelings or beliefs we possess about our being, is almost beyond description and I see such an unconditional offering as an attempt to remind us that tolerance, compassion and forgiveness are gifts which we need to learn to receive before being able to give the same to others.

I recognise part of my task is to facilitate the passage of this pure energy through walls of self depreciation, mistrust and fear which have often been built up over many lifetimes. Through love and respect, I encourage the creation of a sacred space where the dimensions can merge and true healing can occur within the rainbow rays of life-enhancing energy.

And did those feet in ancient time
Walk upon England's mountains green?
And was the holy Lamb of God
On England's Pleasant pastures seen?
William Blake, *Milton,* **1804–1810**

So as to complete the setting, I offer some of my own early spiritual experiences which I now recognise as significant signposts on my intuitive journey.

I entered this world in the mid-50s as peace and hope were permeating the planet. In retrospect, I know that I never lost my connection to the Spirit World and, even as a young child, I recall that on falling asleep I would find myself in a warm bright tunnel which offered great comfort although I had no understanding of its source or why it was so important. As I grew older, the same experience started to occur in meditation and I now associate this place with feelings of tremendous love, soul connection and expansion into the multi-dimensional levels.

I was blessed to be part of a family which was open-minded and where it was not uncommon for our house to be the venue for interesting discussions on esoteric matters, UFOs and *fringe* medicine as complementary medicine was then known. Being born in Britain offered me the opportunity of entering a well-established spiritual tradition where the mystical was expressed through some of the most dedicated, modest and well-respected individuals in the country.

Through the Spiritual Association of Great Britain, I was fortunate as a child to listen to some of the finest examples of trance mediumship (channelling) and to be present at memorable psychic events. The rather undemonstrative way in which many of these talents were revealed is typical of the British reserve, but behind this shield beats a heart deeply spiritually connected to sites such as Stonehenge, Avebury, Glastonbury and Iona as well as the magical crop circles, and represents the peoples' commitment to being guardians of this *Sacred Isle*.

My mother's friend, Joan, was a healer and I see her as a steady, reliable influence on my evolving spiritual life, especially in the field of health care. She never tried to convert others to her belief system but anyone who knew her could only be deeply impressed by her dedicated service, great empathy and wonderful gift of listening.

During my medical training, my focus was understandably directed towards extremely scientific data which was learnt almost parrot fashion. Joan was my salvation, keeping my inner knowledge alive and reminding me that the true vocation of a doctor is never to stop searching for ways of bringing relief, care and hope to those who seek help. While I was in college she developed a malignant tumour of the breast and was determined to treat it naturally, although she agreed to a lumpectomy if she could be given just a little more time to improve her overall health.

She quickly became an expert on every form of therapy which was available. Her home became a natural healing centre with jars of growing wheatgrass filling the kitchen one week only to be followed by pounds of grapes which she consumed with contentment as part of a different diet. Although she herself had cancer, she saw this as a marvellous opportunity to help others and was eager to share her experiences.

Enthusiastic to try everything, Joan and my mother travelled to the Philippines to meet the psychic healers who were attracting so much attention at that time. The English group comprised of many who were terminally ill and were perhaps making this journey as their last hope. Whatever one may think about exploitation, each had free will and my mother recalls atmospheres electric with humour, acts of great selfless-ness and a sense of unified purpose.

When Joan returned for the lumpectomy, the surgeon was surprised to find that the tumour was now benign and had the grace to tell the medical students that this case had received a *'little outside help'*.

Many years later the tumour recurred and this time the cancer spread quickly around her body. On the day before she died I visited her in hospital; even with laboured breathing her sense of humour never waned. As I was re-arranging her pillows she grasped my arm and with a sly laugh said, *'as they are lowering my coffin into the grave, I'll sit up and say "I've thought of another cure"'*. What courage and strength of purpose!

She was greatly missed when she passed but her determination and inspiration are etched in my heart and mind for ever.

Pre-cognition

Despite being surrounded by so much love and encouragement as a child, life was not always easy as my sensitivity and inner knowing exposed feelings, thoughts and images of the future which were not mine but which often left me confused and believing in some way that I was responsible for the people concerned.

Such pre-cognition can feel like a burden unless the acquired information can be used in a positive manner. Indeed, I have met many people who received messages and warnings of imminent events, often in their dream state, who were so terrified by the sense of impotence they evoked, that they switched off all psychic awareness and indeed became very sceptical about the whole subject.

I do not believe that psychic abilities require us to take on the suffering of others or that in order to understand someone else's inner processes it is necessary to sense it in our own body. Both actions can often leave the receiver drained and unable to differentiate between their own feelings and those who seek their help. Psychic abilities are exceptional tools, supplying us with valuable information but this needs to be taken to an intuitive level where clarity of thought and compassion enable us to respond in such a way that all will benefit to some degree.

For my own part, I have learnt to appreciate that I can't carry the world on my shoulders and, in the presence of prior knowledge, I now sit quietly, sending out light and love to all those concerned.

Living in the twilight zone

Physically living with a foot in either world, and not entirely grounded in either, caused me to be prone to severe travel sickness, extreme sensitivity to strobe and flashing lights and to poor spatial appreciation of my own physical body. On the plus side, I was, and still am, very fortunate to have an excellent appreciation of balance and direction, a photographic memory and highly attuned senses.

As I have settled more comfortably into my incarnation, many of these problems have eased and I can now recognise and help others whose developing sixth sense may be disturbing their energetic equilibrium.

Kundalini flushes

Another early sensation which I appreciate now as *kundalini* inspired, was to experience a rush of energy rising up my spine which would evoke a shiver and I would comment that '*someone has just walked over my grave*'. I came to understand that this feeling was very similar to an orgasmic episode and that both symbolised the union between ourselves and our Creator. The experience continues to this day and I recognise that it occurs when there is a realisation from the depth of my being, excitement around an important event, total soul connection or when I am party to spontaneous acts of selflessness.

The kundalini is the serpent energy which slumbers at the base of the spine waiting to awaken and rise to the place of wisdom at the top of the head. This occurs briefly during a sexual orgasm but more slowly and permanently through the inner development of the soul. In ancient times, sexual intercourse was not attempted until the individual had learnt to control this serpentine energy which, symbolising the will, has the capacity to be both a creative and a destructive force. When the snake danced to the song of the soul, forsaking that of the ego, then the individual was allowed to enter a sacred relationship and use the sexually created energy for personal healing and purification as well as contributing to Universal consciousness.

In most Western cultures we seem to have turned these ideas upside down, using the prowess of sexual performance to enhance our ego rather than to dissolve it. Perhaps the increasing levels of infertility, impotence and sexually transmitted diseases are encouraging us to review the purpose of intercourse and to wonder whether it involves more than just procreation of the species.

Disassociation

Finally, I remember that on many occasions I was subject to disassociation where I would leave someone and enter my own home whilst still having an awareness of walking down the street with them. This skill often manifests in those who are learning to move between the dimensions although you run the risk of never existing fully on any one level or of using disassociation to avoid difficult situations where confrontation would be more appropriate.

The future requires us to be able to maintain open access to the multi-dimensional signals whilst focusing on and developing that which is important *now* which includes supportive relationships, a state of well-being and a secure financial base.

As the human mind is adapting to meet these extra demands, I am aware of far more individuals who are having difficulty containing these energies which may manifest as epilepsy, mental illness or in the form of a brain tumour. However, this expansion of consciousness and increased efficient functioning of the brain **will** continue for the sake of human and planetary evolution and can be eased through the release of old beliefs and stagnant emotions which limit the creative performance of the mind.

Our children carry the knowledge of our future and the ability to make it happen. There is a real calling for parents, teachers and others who are connected to the Universal Truth, to reach these souls before they forget how to dream, play and believe that they are invincible!

The planet and its inhabitants are already committed to a tremendous shift in consciousness which will span every section of the community; from education to politics, from health care to families, from religion to environmental issues. As individuals, we are being offered the opportunity to resonate with this new vibration and to awaken to the full potential of our soul.

To conclude this and subsequent chapters I am offering an exercise or meditation which can enhance the interactive quality of the journey by providing deeper understanding and integration. They may be read to you by someone else or slowly to yourself. It is good to keep a journal of your thoughts and observations.

Meditation: expanding the vision

Making yourself comfortable, close your eyes.

Imagine you are standing at the foot of a tall mountain.

Become aware of the scenery which surrounds you; for some this may be houses or village life and for others, trees, meadows or scrub land.

Allow your senses to appreciate the various colours, aromas and sounds around you.

Feel the sun or wind on your arms and face and the solid ground beneath your feet.

You see a path winding up the side of the mountain and decide to take it.

The walk is relatively easy and your spirit becomes lighter as you climb higher and higher.

You are now looking down on the houses and trees which seem far away.

And you continue to climb.

Animals and birds may meet you along the path and accompany you for a little while.

Then suddenly the path is almost obscured by mist and cloud and you become anxious.

But deep inside your inner guidance encourages you and, just as suddenly, you pass through the cloud and burst into brilliant sunshine feeling the life-giving force of the sun all around you. And you continue to climb.

As you reach the summit you can see for miles around.

Spend a little time looking towards the North, East, South and West.

Your vision is unlimited and from here you can gain a different perspective of the journey you have just taken. Looking back at the cloud it now appears so small and insignificant.

You can also see the valley down below and from this elevation can start to understand the life which exists for you at that level.

The top of the mountain provides you with a tremendous sense of freedom and the knowledge that there are no **external** limits preventing you from reaching your full spiritual potential.

Keeping these thoughts in mind, it is time to leave the summit and make your way down the path.

As you descend, you acknowledge that your vision has been expanded and your heart opened and on reaching the valley again you feel great contentment and inner peace.

When you are ready, open your eyes and make a note of any thoughts and sensations which occurred during the meditation.

2 Preparing the way

Give me my scallop-shell of quiet,
My staff of faith to walk upon,
My scrip of joy, immortal diet,
My bottle of salvation,
My gown of glory, hope's true gage,
And thus I'll take my pilgrimage.

Sir Walter Ralegh, *The Passionate Man's Pilgrimage,* **1604**

So we are ready to begin our journey. We've unearthed our universal passport, packed the bags and have set our sights on learning to recognise and trust our intuition so that eventually it can be completely integrated into our consciousness.

The introduction has provided us with a fundamental appreciation of the way ahead so that our mind is already anticipating some of the highlights and challenges of the journey, although many of the details have been deliberately brushed over so that inspiration and understanding can develop, without preconceptions. As we become reacquainted with our guide, the intuition, we experience a deep sense of familiarity as it shares with us some of its extensive background. We come to understand that although we will be supported throughout our journey, there will be certain times when we appear to be alone. It is then that the greatest breakthroughs will occur.

The next step is to learn the ways through which the intuition will make contact and navigate us along the path. Much of the instruction will be delivered as clues or subtle messages which will encourage the senses, especially the sixth sense, to become more receptive whilst also stimulating areas of our brain which have been inactive for far too long, due to our relatively superficial appreciation of life.

Whether the signs emerge from our inner or outer world, their purpose is to produce a vibration which will resonate with our own truth and hopefully leave us in no doubt as to their relevance. The intuition rarely expresses itself through emotional outbursts or by demanding our allegiance via a series of *'shoulds, musts, oughts'*.

It brings all its compassionate wisdom to bear when making clear and concise suggestions whilst leaving the decision to follow through totally in our hands, although there is no promise that the message will not be expressed in many different ways in the future!

There is indeed an attitude which amounts to *'take it or leave it; it really doesn't matter to me'*, which can be a little off-putting when most of your decisions in the past have been as a result of an emotional reaction to other peoples' opinions.

Then there will be the question: *'How do I know it's my intuition and not just my imagination?'* I usually reply: *'Your imagination is the first step towards listening to your intuition and hence follow it as far as you can, whilst keeping an eye open for signs from your inner wisdom that will tell you when to change direction'*.

So, when we find ourselves at a major cross-road on our journey or feel we are stagnating or even lost, we can reach for these access points to our intuition, remembering that:

- The solution may not always be as we expect
- In the end it is not the information which is relevant but our willingness to trust the wisdom of our inner guidance
- It is important to follow the flow of energy through to its completion . . . and then let go and move forward with a new impulse

There will be times to sit, to just be and to pray, appreciating the power of stillness, and then there will be times when we need to rise, to act and become a spiritual pilgrim. Life is concerned with finding unity through polarity and the following suggestions will hopefully facilitate the realisation of this goal.

First we need to be able to recognise our own personal intuitive signals which may be physical, psychological or energetic and include:

- Tingling up and down the spine
- An involuntary shiver or flush of warmth over the body
- Tingling or pressure on the top of the head or base of the skull
- Warmth or pressure over the heart or third eye
- Heat, vibration or *butterflies* in the solar plexus
- A *feeling* that things *'are not right'* often accompanied by the signs given above
- An *inner strength* which cannot be denied
- A *sense of knowing* or *rightness* from the depth of the soul

And finally the: – *'Ah-ha.'*
                      'Of course.'
                      'I always knew . . . '
                      'It just feels right.'
                      'Yes!'

Methods to access the intuition

Alas! I have not hope nor health,
Nor peace within nor calm around,
Nor that content surpassing wealth
The sage in meditation found.

Percy Bysshe Shelley, *Stanzas Written in Dejection, near Naples,* **1818**

Meditation

The benefits of meditation have already been discussed and yet words can never express the impressions which arise from every sentient part of our being as we receive the incoming impulses of our soul and pass through the dimensions to unify with the Creator.

Even though meditation is best practised with mindful awareness of one's posture, breath and thoughts, many people experience glimpses of this state when their left brain is preoccupied with a repetitive action and their right brain, through which the intuitive impulses pass, is open and receptive.

Activities such as washing up, ironing, showering, shaving, gardening and walking the dog are perfect for contemplation which makes me wonder whether the increasing demand for meditation groups is partly due to labour-saving devices! I could add driving to this list for this commonly inspires reflection, but I don't encourage meditation whilst at the wheel as it is preferable that your left brain is in control, especially when you're travelling anywhere near me!

Meditation lowers brain wave activity bringing it in harmony with the rhythm of our Earth Mother and enhancing the healing of the body, mind and spirit. In truth, it is a dynamic process and the stronger our connection to our soul essence through the intuition, the more meditation becomes a way of life rather than something which needs to be accommodated into our daily routine.

Visual Imagery   This active form of meditation presents us with a series of images or scenarios which evoke memories, deeply buried thoughts and pearls of wisdom, allowing them to enter our consciousness so that we can work with them or purely acknowledge our own inner truth.

Our intuition finds this a very favourable way of linking with us as the process requires us to stretch our limits of comprehension so that we can fully appreciate the ingenious nature of the message.

Everybody has the capacity to visualise although the results will be dependent on whether the main modality through which we sense the world is visual, auditory, kinaesthetic, olfactory or gustatory. Since a larger proportion of the population is visual, there has been a tendency to produce meditation exercises based on this modality although it is not uncommon for people to access other senses during a session.

Visual imagery relies on the same network of nerves which allows us to fantasise, day dream and use our imagination. If these have, in any way, been suppressed during our formative years then visualisation may be difficult, as the left logic brain will have been programmed to scrutinise every single thought rather than allow any spontaneous bouts of creative thinking!

Sometimes the images from our subconscious can cause distress and we may try to remove them from our mind, and yet **nothing comes to the surface unless we have the tools to deal with the situation** which, I might say, is just as true for life events. So, I suggest that before you start the imagery exercise you lay beside you a writing journal or drawing pad so that on completion of the session you can record any impressions you received.

It isn't always necessary or appropriate to interpret the results right away and it is often beneficial to hear the insights from a friend whom you trust and respect. In truth, even if we choose to dismiss the experience, any emotional responses which arise will act as a catalyst and start a process of transformation deep within our being.

The meditations which I offer at the end of certain chapters are, in fact, visual imagery exercises but please feel free to use any modality to access your intuition.

Dreams

*I do not know whether I was then a man dreaming
 I was a butterfly,
or whether I am now a butterfly dreaming I am a man.*
Chuang-tzu, Chinese philosopher. 369–286 BC

Dreams have always been seen as a way in which the soul can speak to the lower self. Most dreams occur in the astral plane of existence where there is no finite time or space and where there is a rich source of emotional fuel. This is the same level of consciousness in which psychic sensitivity occurs and therefore those with well-developed psychic awareness tend to be more in tune with their dreams.

In Epidaurus, in Greece, the priest healers recognised the power of dreams and gave powerful potions to their patients before settling them down to sleep in the temple. On awaking, any dreams would be documented with the benefit of expert analysis and then performed by professional actors in a magnificent amphitheatre where the patient had the advantage of being part of the audience.

In this way, they became an objective observer of their subconscious, imitating the role of the intuition and more capable of understanding the meaning of the dream in relation to their soul's purpose.

The great psychologists of the early part of this Century recognised the wealth of information available to us through dreams although, in retrospect, interpretation is probably best left to the dreamer. There are many people who fail to recall their dreams and may even deny their existence. Yet we know everybody dreams so in preparation, before falling asleep, we can ask our inner guidance to help us to remember the experience.

I have met a number people who switched off their awareness after a terrifying dream or after being told to 'stop fantasising' and 'live in the real world' (whatever that means!). It is now becoming more and more apparent that dreaming is an essential tool for total well-being and works on many levels including:

1 **The ability to release from the mind excessive information** from the short term memory bank which would otherwise overload the system. Here the dream is often chaotic and involves people who would normally not be found in the same vicinity. The activities of the night can be exhausting especially if you try to disentangle the confusion. *Just let it go!*

2 **The opportunity to bring to the surface a subconscious concern and receive the wisdom of the soul.** I know for my own part that if I need to hear a specific message, I am woken from my sleep either at daybreak or I wake early and doze for an hour or so and in that time enter a vivid dream state which is subsequently easy to recall. Many of these thoughts stay with me well through the day until I am fully aware of their meaning.

It is common to recognise people in our dreams and then believe that any message relates to them. However, remember that this is our dream and, on most occasions, we are simply being shown an aspect of ourselves which is reflected in the other individual. The same analogy applies to objects and events which are being shown to us as a reflection of part of our nature. e.g. A house usually represents the place in which our soul dwells, and water our emotional state. On recall, it is often helpful to dialogue with these objects to elicit their significance in our lives.

If your sleep memory is not as active as mine, it is useful to have a pad and pencil at your bedside so that immediately on waking you can make notes before allowing the mind to focus on the day ahead. Try to write down all the little details including adjectives and your feelings, for these contain the essential energy within the message. It may be useful to ask someone else for their thoughts on your dream but bear in mind you are the source of the account. It is also fun to find someone with whom you can share your dreams on an on-going basis, a *dream partner*, where together you can share, grow, and offer support.

3 **Meeting someone with whom there is disharmony or unfinished business.** Sometimes it can be difficult to resolve an issue face to face even when the time is right. Therefore, before falling asleep, ask your inner wisdom for the chance to meet this person in your dream state and allow both souls to engage and communicate without the interference of the personalities, hopefully finding a solution to the problem.

4 **The means by which we can travel through the dimensions** often meeting members of our soul family or loved ones who have passed over. Once again, this can be a time for completing personal business or for saying things which had been left unsaid. On many occasions the individual from the spirit world appears younger and in full health with none of the physical problems they endured before leaving this Earth. This insight can lead to a wonderful sense of completion and gratitude as we recognise the transient nature of the physical form in relation to the greater picture.

On waking we may just recall a sweetness, a sense of peace or a familiar scent and fail to remember the powerful encounter of the night.

5 **Travelling to places where we acquire knowledge** which is not available to us on this earth plane but which helps us to be more

effective in our daily lives. At the same time there is an exchange of information where we share with the non-physical world the wisdom of our experiences, adding to the collective consciousness of that group.

This, of course, invites the question as to the origin of those we contact, seeming to need to make a distinction between Spirit guides and Extra-terrestrials. In my mind, we have all been extra-terrestrials at some time and will return to that state on our death. Whether our soul incarnates onto other planets, within other galaxies or even into other Universes seems to be highly probable for, if the Greater Plan is dependent purely on those on Earth manifesting spirit into matter, then it could take a long time!

Many of these dreams fail to reach conscious awareness on waking, apart from a vague memory of being somewhere far away, mainly because our logical brain has difficulty integrating and verbalising the experience. So the information is stored deep within our subconscious where it slowly seeps into our daily thinking, via the intuition, and appears as an inspired thought with no apparent link to our present situation.

6 **Psychic Attack** where you encounter the disruptive energies of another being within the astral realm. These dreams can be very alarming and vivid but usually there is a part of you which is on guard and protects you from real damage. They need to be distinguished from a nightmare where, in the case of the latter, the content tends to relate to something which was present in the waking state, such as watching frightening events on the television.

Psychic attack will be discussed in greater detail in a later chapter.

7 **Lucid Dreaming** which is a subject which is gaining much attention at this moment and is described as the ability *to know you are dreaming while you are dreaming*. Experienced individuals in this field possess clear insight, correct orientation, excellent powers of reasoning and can carry out voluntary activities which were agreed upon before going to sleep. For example, a sleeper may

decide that when they become *conscious* of themselves in the dream, they will perform certain eye movements which can be measured by an observer.

I have experienced brief moments of lucid dreaming, mainly during unpleasant dreams when I was consciously able to divert the course of events towards something less distressing. This ability to use one's will to manifest or remove objects or events whilst asleep reflects our creative skills in the awake state, and is probably helping to dissolve the mental wall of illusion which divides our physical and psychic experiences.

The other feature of this gift is to be able to defy that which is logical within the molecular world so that, not only do we *fly* in our dreams but we *know* we can *fly*, and can consciously manifest this as part of the dream. As we hover above the Earth, we are changing our perception of life from that built on past experience to that which is in tune with our full spiritual potential.

8 **A pre-cognitive dream** is one where information becomes available concerning future events. As discussed previously it is wise to send Light and Love to those involved and be aware that the events may not manifest exactly as revealed in your dream, but may be a symbolic representation, i.e. a death may reflect the completion of a phase rather than physical demise.

9 **A mystical journey** where, within the Light, we experience pure love, the beauty of total connection and the ability to know ourselves completely. This state of bliss exists within us all, the challenge being to manifest it fully within our daily lives.

Nature

Many indigenous races depend on the nature kingdoms to relay messages from the spirit world to the tribe or the individual, each race understanding that they have a different contribution to offer Mother Earth. So we observe that the Australian Aborigines believe that they are one with the land, whilst the Native Americans see themselves as guardians of the planet, working in harmony with all aspects of the Natural World including the four elements and the mineral kingdom.

These cultures, who are so in tune with the rhythm of the Earth, find it strange that those in apparently developed countries have abandoned this connection and tend to treat any non-human form as a second class citizen. Yet many of our 'old wives' tales' rely on an ability to read the messages of our environment, including the nesting habits of birds, the colour of the sky, the direction of the winds and Nature's attempts to supply food in a hard winter by producing bushes laden with berries.

The Animal Kingdom   Many of the ancient races believe that we are all connected to a certain species of animal, bird or insect which is then known as our *totem* animal and that, as we resonate intimately with it's vibration, we receive our most reliable intuitive messages through this source. A shamanistic journey begins by evoking the animal ally through meditation and asking that it will travel with the pilgrim, providing support and guidance along the way.

Already you may be acquainted with this friend and guide, either in a physical form or through your inner world, feeling secure whenever you are in its presence (even though others may consider it to be a dangerous animal). It will often appear at times when you ask for help along your path, providing you with the qualities it possesses to ease your way. e.g. strength (lion), wisdom (owl), dolphin (joy).

Which species of the animal kingdom do you feel drawn towards?

For my own part, even as a small girl, I have been fascinated by snakes and remember that during a trek in the out-back in Australia, a snake suddenly emerged from behind a rock and slithered right between my legs, stayed there for a few moments and then disappeared into the desert again. I felt totally at peace even when the ranger told me that, despite its modest size, *my friend* had a fairly poisonous venom!

Remember that the animal may not always appear to you in a *live* form but may prefer to attract your attention by appearing on advertising boards, on book covers or as the name of a popular product! Such concepts may require you to suspend your rational mind for a moment, but I suggest that you're missing a powerful source of connection with your intuition if you disregard the animal kingdom.

The Plant Kingdom Trees also have a special part to play on our journey. Apart from the strength they impart when we lean against them, and the assistance they offer to ground us through their powerful roots, each tree has its own particular quality as seen in the *Bach Flower remedies*.

There may also be a particular flower to which we are attracted and find ourselves bringing this home whenever we need cheering up or when it's time to celebrate. As with music, our various moods require different frequencies of colour and vibration, which are naturally offered by the plant kingdom. At present, there is a rapidly expanding interest in *flower essences* from around the world, which reflects the intimate relationship which is developing between mankind and this wonderful kingdom.

The Mineral Kingdom The mineral kingdom has always been linked with the mystical, either through stone circles or through the crystal ball of the fortune teller. But its real contribution is only now coming to light.

The stones hold the secrets of our origins; like crystals, they are able to retain the vibration of thought and release it when the correct signal is given. The time has come for the stones to begin to talk. Our ancestors saw the mineral kingdom as the perfect place to store their knowledge as they knew that man's greed would ignore these non-precious stones, preferring the wealth of gold and silver.

It is time to awaken to the true origin of our species and accept our role as co-creators of this Planet and as major contributors to the Universal Plan. The mineral kingdom is willing to open the doors to its *library* if we approach it with genuine respect, honour and humility. So, next time you sit on a favourite rock, in a special cave or within a sacred site, create a moment of stillness and lay aside your expectations. Then open your heart and mind and offer yourself as a messenger for your ancestors and, maybe, you will hear the stones speak.

Another view of the mineral kingdom's role in expanding human consciousness comes from recent evidence involving stone circles, standing stones and sacred caves. It reveals that these stone formations generate an energy field which, when entered, stimulates the brain to produce identical images, even in different individuals, both within the dream state and in meditation. This suggests that the sacred geometry of the stones and the particular pattern they form, plus the underlying *ley lines* (lines of energy within the Earth), provide the perfect setting for stimulation of the mind, especially those areas concerned with symbolism, intuition and, probably, with inter-dimensional communication.

Sacred Space   Wherever we live, Nature, including the sun, moon and stars, is forgiving, non-demanding and ever present. I am sure there is a certain place you go to when you need to think, find space or just relax. You may even have a particular tree, stretch of water or rock which always appears to welcome you and, when you voice your thoughts, seems to be able to provide a sacred space for your own answers to surface. Even when you visit this place in your mind, the same sense of stillness, security and certainty emanates.

If you can't think of anywhere specific, wait until the nature kingdom calls you . . . don't force it. Some people may dowse or use a pendulum but it is preferable to become your own dowsing rod, allowing your energy body to take you to places which resonate with your soul essence. The exercise at the end of this chapter will assist you in finding your sacred space.

I have learnt much from the nature kingdoms and offer you some of the messages I have received:

- At a time when I was attempting to find my own truth, I was walking through a most delightful garden when the gardener showed me a row of trees which he had planted, hoping to form a solid hedge. However, he was disappointed to find that the task had been more difficult than he had first imagined as the trees insisted on being individuals and hence required constant pruning to keep them in line.

  It suddenly dawned on me that this was my story. I wanted to be an individual but kept cutting myself down to size in order to adapt. Through this insight I became determined to stand in my own light.

- I planted a number of seeds in the garden and then became so busy I forgot to water them. One day I took pity on the wilting shoots and fetched the hose to ease their plight. As the water soaked into the earth, it started to rain. *'Just my luck'*, I thought *'I could have saved myself a job'*. Immediately I received an inner message which said: *'You can't plant seeds of any kind unless you are willing to nurture them'*.

  I realised that due to long hours at work I often neglected ideas which were planted in my mind but which I never gave time to explore. Not only would they fail to grow through my inattention but I knew that my inner creative spark would also start to fade.

We travel far and wide to hear the wisdom of Mentors, Gurus and Masters and yet all around us are some of the greatest teachers in the world if only we take the time to stop, observe and listen.

The arts

The arts, such as painting, sculpture, dance, drama, poetry, music, writing, story telling and song, have always been seen as the means to access the deeper reaches of the mind, mainly by stimulating right brain activity. In traditional forms of healing, the Shamans use drums, drama and dance to induce a trance in their subject in order to reconnect them to their soul essence.

The right brain is known to be associated with the intuition, emotions, creativity and inspiration, which when working in harmony with the logic of the left brain, provides us with the opportunity to function as a conscious spiritual being.

Today many forms of therapy used in hospitals and the community revolve around these modalities especially drama, music and art, and all of them have proved beneficial in promoting a sense of well-being even for a short time.

It appears that the arts have two modes of action:

1 **To evoke memories and emotions.** In the majority of cases, the memories and emotions are positive and will open the door to spontaneous creative thought and the chance to remember times of happiness and joy. At other times, the feelings which surface may be distressing and the individual may require professional counselling. However, their release commonly leads to greater clarity of mind and the freedom to move forward along one's path under the guidance of a stronger intuitive impulse.

2 **To strengthen our link with our intuition and other planes of consciousness.** It doesn't matter if you consider yourself artistic or not, we are all creative in our own unique way.

Whenever you feel blocked, need confirmation on a matter or maybe feel so overwhelmed by ideas that you don't know which way to turn, find a large sheet of paper and some crayons and start to *draw* your feelings, thoughts and aspirations. Don't think about it or attempt to analyse the results until the end, just keep going until you feel naturally it is time to stop. (You could also use clay, sculpture, story telling or writing.)

The very act of expression stimulates your right brain and opens the door for intuitive impulses to flood in. When you have finished, stand back and, without logic or judgement, allow your first impressions to emerge:

- If you were shown this by someone else, what would you suggest it was trying to say?
- If you have a trusted, objective friend, ask for their opinion.
- If nothing comes to mind, put the drawing aside and remember that the intuition now has a clearer picture of your thoughts and therefore will provide suitable guidance when the time is right: **so stay alert!**

Whatever method you choose remember that right brain activity puts us back in touch with ourselves, helps us to see our present situation in perspective and re-establishes our position within the framework of Universal Consciousness.

Our body

Our body is our best friend even though there may be times you may believe it has let you down. It is our sacred temple which acts as the vehicle through which our soul incarnates onto this Earth. It is also one of the most powerful communication points for our intuition for, when the body is in distress, we are usually forced to listen.

Without denying the need to treat the body with whatever form of therapy is pertinent at the time, the failure to recognise the link between mind, body and spirit will always mean that present day orthodox medicine can only provide *first aid* measures.

The messages of certain diseases from a psycho-spiritual point of view are well documented in my book *'Frontiers of Health'* but I suggest a number of ways in which the intuition will express itself:

1 **Through the particular site of the illness.** Ask yourself, without the need for any medical knowledge, what does this organ or system mean to you? What is its function? Could dis-ease in this area have anything to do with your life in general.
   For instance:
- Are you feeling overwhelmed by a particular situation? (*Indigestion*)

- Do you feel unsupported and frightened to move? (*Lower back pain*)
- Is your heart no longer in your work? (*Heart attack*)
- Do you feel blocked and unable to express yourself? (*Constipation*)

2 Through the words you use to describe the illness.
For instance:
- 'I feel as if I'm tied up in knots'. (*Irritable bowel syndrome*)
- 'It's as if I'm carrying the world on my shoulders'. *Are you?*
- 'It feels as if there is a lump in my throat'. *Is there something which needs to be expressed?*

3 Through acknowledging the effects of the illness.
- *What does it prevent you from achieving or attempting? This may be positive or negative.*
- *What would you do if you were well?*
- *What opportunities have presented themselves to you since you were ill?*

    It is usually inappropriate to ask this during the acute phase or in the early stages of an illness but the questions and answers can be considered in retrospect.
    How have you changed or what changes have occurred for the positive, since you were ill?

In the midst of suffering it is often difficult to see 'the cloud's silver lining' but, from the soul's point of view, the illness may be its only way of attracting your attention. Once it has that, the illness has performed its role. Of course, we still have to deal with the consequences but in my experience there is a great tendency to concentrate on what is wrong and fail to notice the positive changes which may be subtly taking place.

    It is natural to do everything in one's power to return to total health but if our actions are based on fear then our recovery will be slow and we will be constantly looking over our shoulder to see if *the illness* is following. By looking ahead, we can concentrate on what we want out of life, and see the illness for what it often represents, *a wake-up call.*

By changing our focus it is far easier to hear the messages of our intuition which are enhanced by the use of imagery, painting and voice dialogue.

Other people

We would need to be very sure of ourselves to move ahead with our intuitive ideas without first trying them out on friends, family and even people we meet casually, recognising that the tone of our voice and our presentation will greatly affect the response:

> *'What do you think of this idea?'*
> *'I'm thinking of doing this but I'm not sure'.*
> *'I suppose you'll think it's illogical'.*
> *'I've got this great idea which I know will work!'*

Nobody else stops our creative flow; if we live in fear of change, failure, success, rejection or the unknown, we will attract towards us people who reflect our own fear and will then blame them for holding us back or being unsupportive.

Change your attitude and this will change the response you receive from others.

And do remember that your *best friend* is often the person who tells you the truth even though it isn't what you wanted to hear!

I call it the *'ouch'* effect for their words resonate deep within and cannot be denied.

The Truth wins through

Another advantage of using people to convey intuitive insights is that they move around. How many times have you met someone at a seminar, on an aeroplane or in a queue and find that they have the next message for you as long as you have the wisdom and patience to listen.

Many years ago, at the start of my journey, I remember meeting a woman who showed me a book written about *Findhorn*, a community in the North of Scotland, which you will see later played an important part in my soul growth. I only met her once and cannot for the life of me remember who was running the seminar which we were both attending, but I do not believe that this *'chance'* meeting, was purely a coincidence.

Finally, on the subject of other people as messengers, I often see that when the intuition is determined to show us the type of individual who is damaging to our soul growth, it will send these individuals in rapid succession with each encounter becoming more and more intense.

Eventually, the penny drops and we say: 'I don't need this any more' or 'It's time to confront this issue'.

And the intuition, and all your spirit family, let out a huge sigh of relief!

The media and other forms of communication

The media plays an important part in our life today, with most of us receiving information from a television, radio, computer terminal, journal or newspaper as a normal daily event. Much of the information will drift by our conscious state and too much of it will enter our unconscious without discernment.

However, there will also be times when you open a paper or tune into the radio when you suddenly sit up, experience tingling up and down your spine, and exclaim: *'Ah-ha'* as something resonates with a distant but powerful impulse from within.

Another way of receiving information is through the post, with that vitally important flyer finding its way into your life. Again there is an undeniable sense of recognition which provides the incentive to follow through on this inner impulse:

'It just feels right' we say, or 'it is just what I need at this time'.

You can always ask your intuition to make it very clear if you should proceed in this matter which may mean that the doors are thrown open wide or that they remain firmly shut. But **please** if you ask for this confirmation:

- **Do not sit and grieve** for the lost opportunity
- **Find excuses** as to why you cannot take up the offer.

To complete this chapter, here are some essential tips for making the journey smoother:

- If you *think* you know where you are going you've got a problem!
- The intuition will often just persuade us onto a certain path and then change the goal.
- The intuition will always find some way of attracting your attention.
- You always get what you need but **not** always what you want.
- It is often our ego which seeks the easier life: *'Don't bother, it's nice here, let's stay!'*

The intuition always comes with an enormous supply of patience, love, support, wisdom and, in my case, humour!

Becoming in tune with nature

Allow yourself at least an hour for this exercise.

It is useful to take a notebook and pencil with you, so you can record the experience at the scene.

Take yourself to a place in Nature where you feel comfortable and at peace.

Request permission from Mother Earth to work within this special place and stand until your senses become accustomed to the sounds, colours etc.

Now ask within that you should be drawn towards a tree, rock or area on the ground, which is in harmony with your own soul essence.

You may find your special place with great ease or you may wish to use your body as a dowsing rod.

To do this, walk around the area, preferably clock-wise, using your left hand (palm down) as a receiver of energy; as you approach your sacred space your hand may tingle or become warm.

When you sense that you have found your particular place, stop walking and make yourself comfortable so you can experience a special form of connection.

Here, in your sacred space, you may find stillness, strength, wisdom, unity, the answer to a question or just be open to whatever arises.

Make a note of any images or thoughts which come to mind.

When you are ready to leave, thank the tree, rock etc. *and quietly leave.*

3 The awakening: stepping out

Awake my soul and with the sun
Thy daily stage of duty run
Shake off dull sloth, and joyful rise
To pay the morning sacrifice

Bishop Thomas Ken, 1637–1714

Wake *up, wake up. It is time to go. You've slept long enough and there's work to be done.* The wake-up call is a common theme of many well-known story lines. Its mythology is ingrained within our psyche and throughout our life there will be various times when different aspects of our soul are called home.

Since the awakening is so important to spiritual man, it seems strange that we continue to sleep, despite persistent urgings from our intuition. Somehow we have managed to persuade ourselves that even though our resting place is stony, damp and detrimental to our health, we are extremely comfortable. Truly, we are masters of illusion!

So what makes sleep so attractive? And where do we go from here?

The first stage of the journey is to awaken to ourselves as a unique individual with thoughts, feelings and aspirations. This concept often challenges our *need to belong* which is a tribal energy emanating from our animal instincts, and which when threatened can engender a deep fear of isolation and rejection. Yet this anxiety is irrational for as social beings we are connected at birth to a blood family, through our spirit to a soul family and through events and time to our friends and partners. We are never alone!

At this moment you belong to many tribes or families where you wear an assortment of masks, uniforms, hats and smiles. Hopefully, these different aspects of yourself interconnect but many people live their lives in boxes, sharing parts of themselves with various groups but never allowing anyone to see the complete picture. I wonder how many of you conceal certain aspects of your inner life in order to maintain your membership of a particular society, tribe or club?

This rather *schizophrenic* existence continues until those parts of our being still in the shadows eventually demand to be brought into the light often triggering the wake-up call. Since major change is commonly resisted, the call may appear in the form of a crisis such as illness, the death of a loved one, redundancy or breakdown of a relationship. Even then, we hold on as our fear of the unknown and of vacating a space or situation which is *uncomfortably comfortable*, brings to the surface all those anxieties around which we have created a belief that somehow we are in exactly the right place!

This status quo will continue until one day the intuitive forces employ more subtle methods. We find ourselves becoming deeply absorbed in a book which has been on the shelf for months, turning on the television at a point of great interest, overhearing a conversation which starts us thinking or, more often, developing an inner unease that all is not well.

And still we may hold on; ignoring the message, preferring to believe that if society/the workplace/the partner/the children were different, everything would be okay. We become hypercritical of a particular situation complaining to anyone who will listen, irritated by the inadequacies of others, overwhelmed by the endless demands, disappointed by the lack of support we receive, apathetic about getting out of bed in the morning and still fail to see that the problem is not in the outside world.

We attempt to hide under the covers or pillows hoping that it is all a bad dream and that soon we will awaken to a renewed sense of commitment to our present existence. But the feeling of unease won't go away.

'*Time to get up*', it insists!

One aspect of ourselves may actually admit to being excited by the brave new world which stretches ahead, whilst another part quivers at what appears to be an enormous step. I can remember occasions in my life where 99% of my being was committed to change while 1% was holding on tightly to the past. Despite its minority position, the latter possessed a extremely loud voice and needed much encouragement to know that its feelings were heard but that now it was time to move on.

Indeed, when working with clients, I often notice that the closer they are to change the more expressive their emotions become almost as a last stand against the loss of power of something which has demanded so much attention up to that moment. I therefore recognise that during this time confusion and frustration are very positive signs of trans-formation.

To avoid isolation in our new position, we often try to encourage other members of the tribe to join us on the adventure, pointing out how wonderful their life would be with such a change of view. But frequently we find that they are quite content and unable to understand why we can't be satisfied with the way things are. And our discomfort persists.

So we attempt to straddle two worlds, the old and the new; and it works for a while, until we recognise that we are trying to be all things to all people in our life and no longer being true to ourselves.

I wonder how many of you are experts at keeping plates spinning at the top of poles even though you are exhausted by this dysfunctional behaviour?

Eventually, we pluck up the courage to step into what I call *the corridor*. This isn't necessarily an unfriendly place but it is the twilight zone, the place between worlds. Here we look back to where we have come from and then search the darkness ahead for a glimmer of light hoping to be shown some indication of our future.

To the outsider it may appear that we are *pursuing an impossible dream* and perhaps we have *taken leave of our senses*. They see us in the corridor, apparently paralysed, going neither forward nor backward and such inactivity often triggers the insecurity of our friends and family who offer kind words of encouragement, useful suggestions and well meaning advice. In some cases they even feel responsible for our predicament, although in what capacity is not always clear.

At some point, someone will say: 'why don't you just come back and we'll carry on as before'. And without a second thought, confirming you are on the right track, you blurt out: 'Oh, I don't want to do that', telling yourself and others that knowing what you don't want is just as important as knowing what you do!

The period in the corridor gives time for reflection, stillness, transformation and the confirmation that we trust our intuition. Some people spend longer than others in this place and my perception is that, as your life becomes more entwined with that of the Universe, the ability to learn to be still and trust may require longer periods in the corridor.

Timing becomes everything.

But, eventually the light at the end of the tunnel becomes brighter and you emerge like a newly transformed butterfly into a glittering scene. Here you meet your next tribe or family, people who speak the same language and *wear the same clothes* as that of part of you which has been hidden for so long and it is such a relief not to need to justify yourself or require a translator.

You recognise so much of yourself in this new group and feel alive, validated and content. That experience continues until one day . . . those old feelings return!

Whenever we withdraw from a group and step into the corridor we are leaving behind a set of rules and standards which have provided much of the security and identity which make up the roots of our being. These roots are based on inherited beliefs, personal experience and inner knowing, the last of which has often been negated in societies which discourage thinking by the individual and reward dedicated commitment to the cultural models.

In civilisations where the history goes back over years, the roots are very strong and provide an assurance which is not easily shaken especially where the traditions have been maintained. Many cultures are held together through a belief which embraces a mystical quality as well as a tradition which has been passed down verbally rather than through the written word. In some societies, the same devotion is applied to the material world which, in its own way, provides the attracting force necessary for the creation of tribal energy.

Problems arise when the focus of worship loses its power, leaving its believers anxious, insecure and searching for something else to believe in. Where intuition and self-empowerment are strong, the individual's world is not shaken by external collapse or the breakdown of a wall of illusion, for their inner strength is eternal and they recognise the essential quality of change.

The emergence of *cults* (as the word suggests) is purely a by-product of the changing face of a particular culture and therefore are not themselves the true focus of fear. It is the disintegration of the tried and tested edifices which is the source of the underlying panic. Some cults will survive and become pillars of the community whilst others will be forced to disband. They are not specific to our times but always emerge when old structures are no longer fulfilling the needs of a society and are beginning to fall from grace.

Such collapse is rarely limited to a nation or continent and, as we pass into the Aquarian Age, we recognise that approximately 2000 and 4000 years ago similar transformations were taking place in the Middle East and in Egypt respectively.

On a global level, we are experiencing cosmic changes which are causing a paradigm shift in our consciousness and making us question our spiritual beliefs, basic principles and moral ethics. Each individual is being asked to search within for their own truth and this may require periods of solitude. But, once we glimpse its essence, we will endeavour to find a place of harmony with others so that together we can be of service to the consciousness of the planet.

As each soul awakens and joins their heart and mind to the Universal Truth any false homage which meets only the needs of a few will quickly crumble.

I have had two profound wake-up calls in my life when I was asked to leave the tribe and a position in society that I knew so well. The first was when I was 28 and before I knew about *Saturn returns*. These occur approximately every 28 years of our life and make us look at our path and ask: *'where am I going and am I following the blueprint of my life-plan?'*

I was coming to the end of my training for General Practice and was very keen to be part of this profession. Yet I knew I wasn't ready to settle, feeling that something was missing from the precious tools that were essential in my medical practice.

My twenties were years of hard work as a junior doctor where I was often expected to be on call for between 80–130 hours per week depending on the rotation. Despite this, I loved my work, found it enriching to be part of such a good team of people and felt privileged to be able to help so many individuals at a time of transition.

In my personal life I was also immersed within the tribe, working hard to fit into my perception of social norms and engaged to be married to another doctor with whom I shared all the same interests, except one: my spiritual life.

'You can't have everything' was a phrase often quoted at that time and yet to deny this part of myself was like cutting out my heart. Fortunately, my inner guidance took control at a time when a large part of me felt overwhelmed by unhappiness but was unable to let go of traditional expectations which *I believed* were being imposed from outside. I now know better.

I found myself applying for a post in New Zealand and when I was accepted I didn't realise how this tiny advert, tucked away in a magazine I rarely read, had saved my life. After my time amongst the Maoris, in a country where the glory of Nature is abundant, my soul was re-charged; I returned to England, broke off my engagement and became a full-time partner in a general practice in Essex knowing that now I was fully equipped.

In an attempt to gain a new circle of friends, I joined a group which organised various events for young people, one of which was a visit to a psychic fair. As I entered the room I experienced a sense of 'coming home' and from there my path opened into psychic development classes and spiritual teachings, all of which reminded me of what I nearly gave away in the desperate need to belong to a tribe which, in retrospect, nurtured such a small part of my total being.

Many years later I was told by those who work with me in the spirit world that they thought the doors had closed on the spiritual part of this life until my journey to New Zealand.

My second awakening occurred when I was 33, which I have discovered is an important time for the soul to truly make its impression on the present incarnation. I was working in a delightful general practice where there was great respect and harmony between the partners, where people were willing to take some responsibility for their own health and where I had been given full rein to run classes in relaxation, Tai Chi and complementary medicine. I had a beautiful house and garden and was financially secure; yet, despite all this . . . I was *dead* inside, feeling frustrated and irritable for no apparent reason.

The previous Spring I had visited Findhorn, the community in Scotland where there is a strong link with the nature or deva kingdoms and where pioneers in the spiritual movement often give seminars. I had decided to attend a Natural Medicine Conference and started to make plans trying to decide whether to drive the 600 miles, take the train, or fly, which would be a real luxury. Back and forth I went in my mind and, even when I did decide to fly, I debated long and hard whether to travel in the morning or afternoon.

Eventually, I arrived at the airport to join the other 120 passengers for the flight to Inverness. As I settled into my seat, I asked the girl next to me where she was going: 'Findhorn' she replied. This was Caroline Myss who was one of the main presenters at the Conference. Talk about synchronicity! Knowing in retrospect how important this meeting was for me, I can just imagine the Universe trying to keep up with my change of plans. *'Will she never decide?'* I do hope Caroline wasn't too affected by my dilemma!

Having so enjoyed our conversation on the plane, I naturally signed for her workshop and the following day found myself sitting in a semi-circle where we had to introduce ourselves to the group. I was the last to speak and something happened to me as I waited for my turn for, when I was asked my name, I blurted out through a flood of tears 'I can't go on'. The room was silent but for a small voice inside my head which simply said 'Leave then'.

In the manner typical of the intuition the answer was provided without emotion, pleading or conditions, opening a window to the vast number of possibilities available and leaving me to work out the details. For the next week I wandered amidst the tall, gently swaying Scottish pine trees which crown the hills of Forres, planning the sale of my house, what to do next and how to leave the practice for, in this profession, to leave is like breaking a marriage.

It was a glorious Spring evening when I arrived home and I stood in the middle of my garden beneath the sweetly smelling blossoms listening to the birds sing and thought 'I'd be mad to leave all this. I've just been to some crazy place where they speak to plants and I'm going to give up all my training, my position in society and comfort for what? Nobody knows what happened in Findhorn, I could just go back to work tomorrow and pretend it never happened'.

Instantaneously, I received a past-life flashback which left me in no doubt of my future path. I saw myself in a long line of people going down to the Nile. Those who turned to the right returned to Cairo and to the old ways, whilst those who turned to the left went to join the Sun Pharaoh, Akhenaten, whose believers followed the one God. I saw myself turn to the right and, as I stood in the garden, I heard a voice inside ask: 'Are you going to make the wrong decision again? Have you got the courage to do things differently this time?'

From that moment, I stepped forward with certainty. The following day I announced my departure to the partners who said: 'We knew you would leave some day. How can we help you?' I placed my house on the market and it was bought almost immediately by one of the Estate Agents for his own family. I finally said goodbye on the day after the *Harmonic Convergence*,* little understanding how important this

---

* The Harmonic Convergence was an astrological and spiritual event which took place in August 1987 when most of the planets of our solar system formed between them a *Grand Trine* or triangle. This was seen to be a very auspicious occasion by many of the Ancient Peoples including the Tibetans and Hopi Indians and represented the opening of a door to a new level of consciousness upon this Planet.

time was for planetary consciousness and stepped into a life which has brought richness, love, wonderful connections, travel, ever expanding knowledge and a sense of being on the right track.

Past life regression has become popular recently. For my part, I have always found that I receive information when it is necessary and usually when I can change an old karmic pattern.

Whether or not one believes in past lives, or thinks that they emerge purely from an over-active imagination, is personal, but the pertinent question has to be: '*What are you going to do with this information?*' Knowledge from regression therapy should never be used to disempower the soul or be used as an excuse for inactivity.

There are very few *new* souls on the Earth at this time and therefore most of us have many experiences of previous lives. The recall of a particular situation from the past suggests that there is:

- Unfinished business to be completed
- The opportunity to do things differently
- The presence of an important relationship (which may not have the expected outcome)
- A skill which needs to be re-awakened in this life.

In the story recounted above, the past life memory, and the question I was asked, propelled me beyond fear and into an existence where I have none of the regrets which I believe would have been present today had I remained in general practice.

**Regrets are too late when we are on our death bed . . .
live life to the fullest now!**

Such wake up calls may appear to ask us to leave those we love. But most of us have commitments especially to our children and parents and the intuition always attempts to embrace the spiritual needs of others as well as our own inner urgings. There are many today who are awakening to their own truth and mistakenly believe that it is their right to abandon all responsibility.

Unfortunately, when changes are made without consultation, compassion, respect and the acceptance of one's obligations, then we are merely rebelling against the tribe and acting like a *temper tantrum toddler* rather than walking our path with maturity. The break which is required is more often emotional rather than physical and this frees others to live their life in harmony with the eternal song of their soul.

When we give space to the isolated parts of ourselves, we often find that our relationships become richer, deeper and more long lasting. Any connection, whatever the source, which is held together through fear and guilt cannot survive, for love, honour and respect are the adhesive qualities necessary to create meaningful relationships.

Sadly, too many families, partnerships, societies, political parties, nations and businesses are based on negative bonding where the few hold the freedom of the many in the palm of their hand and are unwilling to let go of this control due to their own insecurity and fear of being alone.

Here the *spirit of the group* has been neglected with preference being given to the needs of the individual. In theory, nobody is forced to stay within any group but each person will have their own specific agenda which may be hidden behind an apparently altruistic motive.

> e.g. 'They couldn't do without me' or 'The place would fall apart without me at the helm'.

Even when our families are involved, the selfish action may be to stay, especially when our heart no longer resonates with the tribal note and when staying merely shelters us from loneliness, taking responsibility, accepting the inevitable void or perhaps reaching the full potential of our soul! By letting go of our emotional dependency on the tribe we are able to offer far more spiritually and physically to the overall quality of the group energy.

Many companies in the industrial world are experiencing a trans-formational shift in attitude recognising that competition which is built on fear and secretiveness leads not only to stagnation of productivity but also to poor co-operation between the various departments of the corporation. The time for discussion is over with implementation needing to start at the top of these organisations with those involved recognising their responsibility for raising the consciousness of the business world.

The first step may be appreciating that one's position in society or within an organisation should not negate the simple need to respect others whatever their role. It is often hard for those who are ambitious to understand that there are many people who have found their level of fulfilment and can be very generous from this place of contentment. However, the experience may force us to look within and ask whether or not we are pursuing contentment in the wrong direction, recognising that our *teachers* can take on many guises.

I have a strong image in my mind of a circle of people holding hands which on the surface appears supportive. Yet on closer inspection, the physical contact is unnatural, relying on threats and uncompromising loyalty. The only way forward is for each member of the circle to release their grip and allow the development of new bonds built through:

- Love, respect and honour for each other
- A willingness to take responsibility for personal thoughts, words and actions
- A joint decision to act for the good of the whole rather than for the individual.

Such connections enrich creative expression, intelligence, commitment and productivity and negate the need for unhealthy competition, secretiveness, emotional blackmail and fear. It is a big step to take but many groups and families are seeing it as the only way to producing a happier and healthier world.

There are, of course, situations where team effort is essential and where individual initiative needs to be discouraged such as during emergencies involving the armed forces, police and the fire brigade. However, many members of these groups tell me that they have a highly developed intuition which is a combination of years of experience plus an uncanny sense of inner knowing. In this way, policemen read body language and listen for what is *not* said in order to form an opinion, whilst firemen use their inner awareness to assess which rooms need to be searched, whilst being intuitively conscious of a wall which is about to collapse.

During more peaceful times, the team spirit could be relaxed so as to allow the individual to express their insights as to ways of creating a more efficient service with greater job satisfaction, although it takes a secure and wise leader of the tribe to consider changes which may threaten his or her power.

One of the archetypes who is instrumental in helping us maintain our position in the tribe is called the *protector* who has often come into our life at a very early age. This character may actually be represented in the real world by a parent or guardian but usually appears in our inner world as a sub-personality, at a time of our life when we feel threatened or insecure either physically, emotionally or spiritually. It is possible to access this part of ourselves through work such as *Voice Dialogue* (see Bibliography) or through various forms of visual imagery.

The protector is dedicated to its role in our life and like a program on the computer will only discontinue this task when the software is changed by the operator. It is therefore important to recognise our own particular protector for, until we do, he/she may act in our very best interests and yet sabotage our decision to move on. Like a loyal employee, his/her retirement should be managed with dignity and possibly with the opportunity to continue to serve us in a different manner.

I remember when I met my own protector. He's called *the pusher*. In my younger days, I was painfully shy and tended to stand back, frightened of being noticed. My parents encouraged me but in some ways that only made it worse as I then felt responsible for their predicament.

Enter the protector bearing a powerful set of hands which locked into my back and started pushing me forward. Engaging my own inner driving force, I entered situations which as a child I would have believed impossible.

However, over the years, I started to develop pains in my upper back related to tension especially when my *'in-tray'* was full. I decided to discover the source of this tension and one day in meditation, met the pusher happily fulfilling his task by projecting me in all directions.

'Where are we going?' I asked and he replied 'It doesn't matter as long as we just keep moving!'

I saw we had a problem! So I compromised and with great tact and diplomacy, thanked him for serving me so faithfully throughout my life but explained that now I needed to slow down and take time to be still and contemplative. I suggested that we changed his job description so that he would push away from me all those situations which were not healthy for my soul growth, and push towards me all those experiences which would enhance my being.

Fortunately, he agreed. Since then, the backache has eased, I have taken more time for myself and I have watched with fascination as situations have come towards me rather than my having to go out and look for them.

So who is your protector?
Do they serve your soul or a childlike aspect of your personality?

On many occasions, the protector is embodied in someone close to us or to whom we offer authority. We may not like the position that we are forced to take with them and yet feel unable to move if we want to avoid meeting the challenge of entering unknown territory and possible feelings of isolation. Once we come to understand that this authority figure is actually representing part of **our** sub-conscious and is feeding our fears, we can re-negotiate our terms of agreement with this person which often leads to a change in the relationship and openings for all concerned.

Finally, it is not uncommon to switch from being the one who needs protecting to becoming the one who protects, believing that everybody is dependent on you for their survival. Forming our own tribe can help to reinforce our belief that we are on the right path and yet we can also find ourselves on the loop of illusion if we try to carry anybody except ourselves.

> *'People need me, I couldn't let them down'.*
> *'What would they do if I wasn't there?'*
> *'I would love to break free but* (huge sigh) *you know what it's like?'*

Sometimes we need to be honest and ask 'Who needs who?'
'How would you feel if everybody was happy to manage without you?'

Intuition is always present, providing us with a welcoming beacon in the midst of fear and doubt. But, if our fear of change is stronger than that of staying where we are, we will not change, preferring to close our eyes to the spiritual Light.

Fear and anxiety diminish our ability to respond to inner urgings, stagnating soul growth and separating us from ourselves.

It is easy to recognise that fear often produces an image of the future which is far worse than the reality and that, when we use the same adrenaline drive to excite rather than create anxiety, we are naturally propelled towards those things which bring hope, fulfilment and love.

Ultimately, when we walk along our own path, we engage an inner strength which amplifies our confidence and allows us to develop deeper relationships with our family and friends as we no longer need to wear the cloak and mask.

Our spiritual alarm clocks were set long before we came on to this planet; some of them have been ringing for a long time. *'Wake up, wake up; it's time to go!'*

Awakening exercise

The Spirit of the Tribe:
In your journal, make a list of all the tribes to which you belong.

It is very unlikely that any one group will meet all your needs.

Are there any tribes where you feel that you no longer belong and perhaps where there are on-going tensions or an increasing lack of enthusiasm?

Recognising that, despite your opinion, it is not necessarily the tribe which has to change, ask yourself:

- *What do I need to change in order to bring myself in harmony with the spirit of the group?*
- *What do I need to express in order to feel more in tune with the group?*
- *Is there something I could offer which would increase my commitment to the group?*
- *Is there a moral way that I can meet my needs elsewhere whilst belonging to this group?*
- *What stops me from leaving?*
- *Am I really working for the good of the whole by staying or only meeting my own needs?*
- *What do I need to do to explore other options?*

If you believe that you are in the corridor:
- *Are you comfortable in this position?*
- *Would there be anything which prevented you going back?*
- *Do you know what you don't want even though you're unsure of what you do want?*

- *Is there any anxiety about going forward such as fear of success or failure?*
- *What was your soul's intention before entering the corridor? What are you seeking?*

If you are standing in your own light . . . Congratulations!

4 Expansion: taking on one's own power

*You only have power over people as long as you don't take **everything** away from them. But when you've robbed a man of **everything** he's no longer in your power – he's free again.*

Alexander Solzhenitsyn, *The First Circle,* **1968.**

The initiation which occurs when we step into the corridor reawakens the power which has slumbered for so long under an illusionary cloak of helplessness and our etheric frame expands to encompass the energy that is now available. Like the day we receive our first earnings, we experience concern for its security, a sense of freedom, the knowledge that we now possess bargaining power, a desire to spend wisely and the need to find someone trustworthy who will advise us on investments which will lead to greater joy and fulfilment in our life.

These challenges are similar to those found on this stage of the journey:

1 **Securing the new energy** whilst allowing it to multiply through *creative endeavour.*

2 **Generating further energy** through our connection to the Source rather than by becoming trapped in *power games* where there has to be a winner and loser.

3 **The right use of the energy** with the activation of *psychic powers.*

4 **The willingness to expand consciousness,** opening the way for *greater insight* and *spiritual guidance.*

To assist us along the path, our senses, the means by which we communicate between our inner and outer worlds, become heightened with enhanced appreciation of the richness of colour, greater definition of design, improved tactile sensitivity, more exquisite hearing and an attraction towards the more subtle aromas.

Securing the new energy

The strength gained by courageously following the intuition despite the persuasive nature of the tribe allows our true voice, which has been silent for so long, to be heard. We begin to cherish the ability to make choices and use the 'No' word with more regularity and greater conviction, determined to speak from the heart rather than just going along with the crowd in order to gain approval.

This new stance frequently produces ripples in our environment causing family, friends and work colleagues to feel mystified by the transformation and anxious to know how it will affect them. Some feel threatened and react with comments bordering on aggression or sarcasm whilst others defend their own position even though it was not in question.

But there are those who have taken risks themselves and know the corridor, appreciating the value of space to develop this new sense of Self and recognising that many models may be designed and rejected before we settle on one which reflects the essence of our journey at that time.

On leaving general practice I decided to travel across the USA, visiting holistic health centres run by physicians whom I respect to this day for their pioneering work. As I crossed the Atlantic I believed that my next role was to organise such a centre in the UK and was eager to discover what was successful and what was to be to avoided. Four thousand miles and six months later, after meeting some wonderful people, many of whom were not on my original list, my plans had been refined and transformed. Returning to England, I opened a homoeopathic practice and focused my attention on increasing public awareness of the advantages of complementary medicine whilst working to enhance the understanding of the mind, body and spirit connection.

While we are still experimenting with our inner voice, there is a natural desire to share our enthusiasm and insights with others. One word of advice; at times of vulnerability and change, keep away from *bubble poppers*. You may have met them already. They commonly inhabit supermarket queues, your own living room, the area around the coffee machine at work or the bar of your local pub. They can't wait for some-one to come along with a newly inflated thought bubble and, as you excitedly reveal its contents, they pull out a large pin and pop it:

> 'Well if you want my opinion . . . '
> 'That sounds great but I wouldn't do it!'
> 'Don't come crying to me when it doesn't work'
> 'What do your family/partner/parents/friends think about that?'
> 'Well, I suppose you could always go back to your old job'
> 'You always did have strange ideas'
> 'Don't say I didn't warn you!'
> 'Are you sure you can afford to do it?'
> (To which I reply: 'I can't afford not to!')

Beware of these people when you carry delicate new ideas where the paint is still wet; they are easily recognisable for they carry this large pin and have never felt fulfilled or taken a risk in their lives. They tend to surround themselves with other non-achievers, pretending to be their protector whilst hiding behind this role. And don't be fooled by the images of a successful existence for we all gravitate towards areas in life which come easily and yet can be reluctant to face situations which may be the true purpose of our soul incarnation.

It's not what we do but how we do it

After years of following the tribe it can be quite daunting to realise that your future is dependent on your ability to spend wisely whilst consolidating your personal assets. It soon becomes apparent that there are specific issues which demand attention, linked to an agenda that was set long before you came on to this earth and which have the potential to enhance the consciousness of the incarnate soul.

In theory, the objective appears simple and merely requires us to create scenarios in which these issues can be expressed, produce a response, enable greater understanding and become integrated into the total experience. But somehow we get lost in our own theatre production believing that the purpose of our existence is embodied within the external world and all that it offers in terms of material wealth, social identity and success.

In our eagerness to multiply our own store of personal power it is easy to forget that at the end of this life the most relevant question related to soul growth will be *'how did you live your life?'* rather than *'what did you do?'* This awareness should not lead to fear and inertia but rather encourage us to shift our focus from the needs of the individual to the appreciation of the inter-connectedness of life, recognising that it is the **manner** of our relationships which fashions our world, not the **substance**.

Recently I was listening to Professor Kenneth Ring, who is an expert in Near Death Experiences (NDEs). He was talking about the *life review* which is a common feature of the NDE. The contributors to his study spoke of seeing their life flash before them and of having the ability to both sense the relevant emotion and, at the same time, fully understand why the situation had occurred from the perspective of the soul.

From this objective standpoint, judgement and guilt were not the main issues as the over-view often left the subject with a deep sense of regret as they viewed situations which they had either avoided or left unfinished often due to their preoccupation with their own personal plight. They saw times when they had been offered the chance to experience new horizons and instead had scorned those who welcomed them with open arms and other occasions when kindness had been requested and they had remained aloof.

In some cases, the individual was given the opportunity to appreciate not only their own feelings but also the emotions of those who had suffered pain or abuse at their hands. This profound insight into the inner process of someone else often culminated in a totally new way of interaction after the NDE, where the individual considered the sentiments of others rather than immediately reacting or basing their behaviour on their own fear of losing control.

Others realised that through their own self-protection and a misguided concern for those they loved, they had failed to speak or act, leading to stagnation for all concerned. Intuition asks us to look beyond our own personal needs and see the whole picture, allowing us to perform for the benefit of all souls involved, even though our actions may not be totally understood at the time.

Finally, on the matter of securing energy, we are more likely to give our power away or become spiritually impoverished when we take ourselves too seriously, allow fear to obstruct the natural flow or fail to see the larger picture. We are purely guardians of this energy; we don't own it nor should we fear its loss. By accepting the eternal flow of energy which converts spirit into matter and matter back to spirit, we are freed from the fear of failure, the fear of the unknown and the fear of death, and can enter a place of stability where wonder and magic abound.

I received a powerful reminder of this message during my first encounter with the dolphins around the idyllic islands of Hawaii. There I was swimming in this wonderful clear, blue water surrounded by these enchanting animals who were unconditionally offering me love, play and an overwhelming sense of belonging and my over-active mind was pre-occupied with problems which I should have left behind in England.

Suddenly one of the dolphins swam right up to my face, looked me straight in the eye and with such tenderness and wisdom spoke directly into my thoughts:

'You're so serious; you keep forgetting;
 . . . nothing matters; everything just exists.'

My awareness of the transient nature of physical existence was transformed from that moment and now whenever I take myself too seriously I remember that since I create the perception of my reality, if I smile, the world smiles back.

Generating further energy

'The human race, to which so many of my readers belong, has been playing at children's games from the beginning, and will probably do it till the end, which is a nuisance for the few people who grow up'.

G.K. Chesterton, *The Napoleon of Notting Hill,* **1874–1936**

As we emerge from the dependency on the group to supply our needs and begin to develop self-consciousness, our energy expenditure increases, forcing us to find a source of power which will restore our dwindling supplies. Our own internal generator was abandoned aeons ago when we became reliant on external reserves to fulfil our requirements. Despite its neglected state, the wiring system is still intact and with an adequate overhaul and a flush of light through its network can once again become the source of infinite power. All we have to do is to remember where to find the switch!

Until our memory returns, like many others we engage in a variety of sophisticated yet subtle power games which originate in the astral or emotional body and which aim to augment our energy supply by manipulating someone else to forfeit a portion of their own personal power. This produces a winner and loser although in the long term the effort involved is spiritually draining for all concerned.

The game employs specific, emotionally fuelled sub-personalities including the *martyr, critic, controller, victimiser, victim, avoider, guilt-tripper* and *pleaser* all of whom are experts in obstructing the flow of the soul's intention which is aspiring to be expressed via the intuition.

These characters have featured strongly throughout the history of man and have been the focus of discussion in many psychology text books. Yet, despite their unsavoury habits, they maintain their control over human relationships, reinforced by a barrage of information from the media which feeds one or more of these archetypes. They thrive on misdirected emotional expression, low self confidence, mistrust of others and on our failure to acknowledge our connection to the source of our being.

A dense cloud has formed around the etheric mantle of this planet through our continual reliance on this source of inert fuel. However, it is starting to break up through the immense efforts of those working multi-dimensionally who are showing us that Light and Love are the only pure forms of energy for spiritual man.

Most of these games are so insidious and addictive that we are genuinely unaware of our participation although very capable of pointing the finger at others. Despite the tremendous variation in circumstances, the aspiring winner employs certain tactics time and time again.

The martyr

- *Accepts every request and challenge without complaint whilst making it very clear non-verbally that praise and appreciation are expected*
- *Sends out distress signals accompanied by much moaning and groaning then refuses the help offered*
- *Silently expects others to meet their needs and feels resentful when they don't*
- *Uses phrases such as 'I'm fine', 'I'll cope', 'Don't bother, I'll do it myself'*
- *Believes life is about suffering and struggle*

The critic

- *Finds fault with others so as to secure their own position*
- *Subtly 'pulls the rug from under the feet of their opponent' often with a back-handed compliment*
- *Finds it difficult to praise (they are commonly just as hard on themselves)*
- *States that they are 'only offering useful advice' even though others crumble under their inappropriate opinion*

The controller

- *Has to have the last word*
- *Must prove their point without shifting their position one inch*
- *Refuses to be the first to say sorry (even though this results in stalemate)*
- *Has to remain in control/on top/in command/apparently strong/ capable*
- *Appears to want to understand whilst listening from a fixed view of reality*

The victimiser

- *Demands allegiance through intimidation and fear*
- *Meets their own needs by threatening the security of others*

The victim

- *Is an expert in avoiding responsibility, always looking for someone else to blame*
- *Believes that things just happen to them and don't understand why*
- *Feels rejected and angry when anybody else demands attention*
- *Starts sentences with global statements such as 'The world is . . . ', 'People are . . . ',*
- *Concludes with 'That's life', 'It always happens to me', 'I thought you cared!'*
- *Persistently asks questions beginning with 'But how?'*
- *Revels in repeating their story without ever seeking insight into its message*
- *Expects others to **know** their needs without providing any verbal clues*

The avoider

- *Avoids conflict or criticism by becoming distant, falling asleep, walking out, taking the dog for a walk, hiding behind the newspaper/television/computer, changing the subject or running out of the room*
- *Makes it difficult for people to love them, demanding more and more proof*
- *Pulls back and erects barriers as soon as anybody comes too close*
- *Becomes extremely busy and unavailable so as to avoid confrontation and the truth*
- *Tempts others towards their secret inner place even though the key was thrown away a long time ago*
- *Misses out on reality by being permanently absent from the centre of their own life through fear of encountering criticism*

✓ The guilt tripper

- *Attempts to prove that **everything** that happens to **anybody** must be their fault!*
- *Confuses care with guilt; 'If I feel guilty it must mean I care!'*
- *Uses remorse to avoid personal growth and expansion of self-awareness*
- *Believes that their actions can truly influence the free-will of another*

The pleaser

- *Requires constant reassurance and approval, which they refuse to accept*
- *Seeks persistent encouragement rather than just getting on with the job*
- *Accepts all requests with a willing smile even though there is inner resentment*
- *Is sensitive to everybody's needs and attempts to meet them **all** without asking for permission*
- *Expresses their displeasure through statements such as: 'I'm not complaining but . . . '*
- *'You would have thought, after all I did for them . . . '*

I wonder if you recognise yourself in any of these statements?

These games are to be found in all sectors of society where the personal power of the individual is used as a means of negotiation. On many occasions the contest takes place non-verbally with words being irrelevant in the face of raised eyebrows or down-cast eyes which convey powerful messages and secure the winning position.

It is time to leave these games behind and open our channels to a flow of energy which nurtures and guarantees the survival of spiritual man. By tuning into the supreme compassion of the heart and the inherent wisdom of the mind we reclaim our birthright. This ensures that:

> **When we are walking our true soul path, the Universe is obliged to respond to our intention by providing us with the energy and the means to transform inspiration into manifestation; spirit into matter.**

If leaving the tribe behind was difficult, giving up the addictive habits of game playing demands much greater willpower, asking us to step out from behind a familiar role and relinquish the benefits we have received, often subconsciously, during most of our life. It can appear almost impossible to disentangle ourselves from the web of illusion and is complicated by our ability to conjure up excellent reasons why we should stay in exactly the same place.

Indeed, we have invested so much time and energy in this character that we have no intention of giving up so easily especially as awareness brings a sense of shame that we have allowed the game to continue for so long; our pride can't cope with the revelation. Of course, we could always start a new game concerning the guilt we now feel at wasting our soul potential. The possibilities are endless!

If we wish to move forward a useful question which demands an honest answer is:

'What do I gain from being a martyr/victim etc.?'

Of course we may be shocked by the suggestion that we are 'attention seeking', 'avoiding responsibility' or 'denying ourselves intimacy' but nothing happens by chance and well-developed patterns must have received generous nurturing over the years.

The intuition helps us to break free of these habits by bombarding us with one person after another who either acts as a mirror of one of our sub-personalities or who has the ability to immediately *call into play* our victim/controller, etc. The hope is that persistent events will accelerate our awareness of the game and eventually we will call a halt. Unfortunately, some individuals don't give up that easily and their guides have to be extremely cunning and patient.

Even when we do choose to change, other people may not offer the support we expect for they are losing a fellow contestant and will need to find someone else to play the other part. Even the critic and controller can be missed for without their authority many feel disorientated and insecure!

But it is only when we appreciate that the game requires at least two players that we realise that if we want to generate additional power we have to stop participating in the contest. On many occasions we are 'found out' by someone who says to the critic: 'Why is it that your comments always sound so critical? I know that this is not your general nature but I find it very upsetting?'

Such a remark often brings about tremendous changes for, as with children who are caught in the act of wrong-doing, most people respond to shame. Even though our pride may prevent us from openly owning these characteristics, the truth always resonates internally and our intuition tells us its time to move on. With our secret habits now out in the open the competition loses it's fun and the liberated energy can be turned towards the true purpose of the soul's journey on this Earth.

Games are unnecessary where there is a healthy self-esteem which develops through the ability to forgive ourselves and release old pains, blame and other redundant emotions. Many believe they are unforgivable and yet, when we acknowledge that we express an essential aspect of the Creator, there is nothing we do which is not part of the whole. Everything is known at some level and, depending on our desire to become responsible for our actions and change accordingly, there will always be a positive outcome for global consciousness.

Enduring self-esteem comes from a genuine belief in oneself, appreciation of the efforts made to walk the spiritual path, graciousness to accept our foibles and the willingness to learn from every experience. With this degree of confidence, we fail to provide the hooks and triggers which are required to qualify for participation in the games. No longer of interest as an opponent, we are able to continue our journey with greater ease, lighter spirit and the freedom to appreciate fully the beauty of life.

Like many others in the caring professions, I have had to juggle with the aspiration to be of service to humankind with the desire to rescue or *fix* everybody I encountered, which ultimately can lead to martyrdom or feelings of resentment. My own profession is an ideal breeding ground for any promising young martyr, guaranteeing that nurturing and care pass in one direction only. Sleep, food and other normal human needs are overruled when the bleep sounds and any sign of dissension is met by elderly colleagues telling you that they worked similar hours in their youth and it's all part of the training.

These words of reassurance and encouragement remain only long as it takes you to consider that, just because it was the practice in the past, we should still be sending young boys up chimneys. Yet, the subtle emotional blackmail in health care is rarely related to threat of redundancy but rather to the more moral standpoint that service requires sacrifice.

I was provided with a salient lesson about attracting towards oneself those things which you believe and how your response inevitably perpetuates the hypothesis. A few years ago a friend telephoned to ask me whether I was interested in a holiday which would involve pure nurturing and no demands. As I stood and listened, I went into my script. 'It is all very well for her to talk; I can't take time off, people need me; I haven't got the time for such luxury!'

As I replaced the receiver, I thought 'Boy, do I have a problem. The martyr seems to be ruling my mind and my life. And worst of all, I really believe what it says!'

The following morning, as I was travelling to work the train pulled into the town where I had practised as a general practitioner seven years earlier and a cry went out *'Is there a doctor on the train?'* Realising that nobody else had moved, I made my way to the carriage where a young girl had fainted. When she was fully revived and I had returned to my seat I acknowledged that it was no coincidence that we had stopped at a location where caring had been so much part of my being.

As we sped towards London I reflected that my role as a rescuer had infiltrated many areas of my life, including my close relationships, where the imbalance in the flow of energy between us was beginning to cause stress and resentment. I knew the answer was in my hands and recognised that over the years I had been called upon to provide assistance to friends and strangers alike which I performed with sincerity. Yet I could see that I was hiding behind this role and needed to find out who I was and the true value of love.

When I arrived at the clinic I gave in my notice and started a whole new phase of my journey, acting from a place of spiritual integrity rather than from the expectations proffered by society. I still care, I still love, but I have learnt the value of healthy boundaries and the wisdom to know that teaching others to listen to their inner guidance and their body's messages is far more valuable in the long term than simply rescuing and fixing everybody.

The right use of the energy: psychic activation

As the developing intuition passes through this stage of the journey our sixth sense, or psychic power, is activated bringing towards us the ability to experience life beyond the five physical senses. We are presented with tools of consciousness such as *clairvoyance*, *clairaudience*, *telekinesis (psychometry)* and *telepathy* which enable us to enter the subtle realms of existence where mysticism, transformation and true connection reside.

Some people are highly gifted in this area, often from childhood, whilst others develop these skills through study and the willingness to be open to new experiences. I was very fortunate to attend *psychic development circles* where the teaching combined the enhancement of one's talents with spiritual wisdom. Here I studied the tools mentioned above plus automatic writing, channelling and the *reading* of subtle energies all of which stimulated my awareness of other dimensions of existence as well as whetting my appetite to know more.

Despite the spiritual blossoming which ensues through psychic development, this heightened awareness can also cause us to feel uncomfortable as we can become increasingly sensitive to atmospheres and other peoples' thoughts and feelings, until we learn to handle this powerful energy.

Psychic awareness is processed through the energy centre called the *solar plexus* (situated in the area of the stomach) which is involved with developing a healthy self esteem and is the seat of our emotions. The solar plexus acts like a large satellite dish scanning the atmosphere for subtle energies and particularly for anything which could threaten the confidence of the individual, relaying the information in the form of feelings.

This centre becomes highly developed in those children who live in dysfunctional households where communication is poor or incongruent, where there is unreasonable anger or where mood swings are common place. Here the child uses its scanner to detect subtle changes and responds accordingly, for survival is the name of the game.

Unfortunately, even after the threats diminish, many adults continue to rely totally on the impulses of this centre, known as *gut feelings*, and fail to listen to their intuitive wisdom. The problem is that the psychic messages which are received are not only reflecting present circumstances but will also tap into any emotions which relate to similar incidents in the past, especially when the self-esteem of the individual was threatened.

For example:

You are introduced to someone who has the same name as a colleague with whom you had serious disagreements in the past. On hearing their name, your gut feelings say: 'remove yourself from this situation as soon as possible'. However, when you stop and listen to your intuition it says: 'Isn't it time you moved beyond this issue, completed unfinished business and enjoyed the encounter with this new friend?'

The children of today are far more sensitive to all levels of subtle communication than in the past and hence more vulnerable to outside influences, especially those on an emotional level. They easily detect the moods of their parents and, in the case of disharmony, can become overwhelmed by their inability to *'make things right'*. They need to be taught how to tap into the guidance of their own intuition rather than being engulfed by their feelings.

Here are some suggestions for a healthy psychic awareness:

1   Create healthy boundaries where your needs for time and space are respected.

2   Learn to 'count to ten' before giving an answer; saying: *'I'll come back to you'*, which provides thinking time.

3   Speak from the heart rather than from a place of fear.

4   Act, not react, responding to the action not the actor.

5   Don't allow the 'gut feelings' to over-ride the insights from the intuition.

Overload

As the psychic powers develop it is important to modify the incoming information in order to prevent overload. Imagine walking into a room and picking up all the sentiments and thoughts that are being expressed at that time. If this happens to you, it is vitally important to close down your psychic powers on entering a room or learn to transmute the excess sensory input so as to avoid burn out.

The latter can be achieved through:

- Sending the energy into the ground and asking Mother Earth to transform it into power-for-good
- Sending it towards the Light and asking that pure Light should be sent to those who need it.

During this phase of development *psychic protection* may be required, especially when entering unfamiliar surroundings, when there is undue stress, or in the presence of someone who easily drains your energy (although recognising their influence over you and plugging the leak is far more effective).

Methods of Protection:

1 Imagine yourself surrounded by white light, which can take the shape of an egg extending beneath the feet. White light contains all the colours of the rainbow and therefore reflects all other energy back to its source.

2 Place yourself in a golden pyramid with a golden floor under your feet. The light enters through the top and all other energies which are not beneficial to the soul are reflected back to their source.

3 Imagine a mirror in front of you with the reflective surface towards the other person. Receiving back one's own energy can have an amazing effect!

4 Visualise the closure of the solar plexus like a flower closing at night.

5 If all else fails, do what feels natural and fold your arms across your solar plexus.

As the psychic powers become more manageable and the soul's note becomes stronger protection develops from within and the methods mentioned above are then only required on specific occasions. Psychic protection corresponds to wearing a *plaster cast* over a broken leg, providing security while the bone mends. However, when healing is complete, the cast must be removed otherwise movement will be hampered. Persistent use of the white light obscures the infinite power of our inner light and suggests that the world outside is never to be trusted and has the potential of attracting towards us those things which we most fear.

One of the greatest inner strengths is the ability to come from the heart. Whenever I am in unfamiliar surroundings, I purposely move my awareness into my heart and feel the flow of love and peace towards myself and towards those I encounter. The response has been remarkable and works particularly well when encountering unfamiliar animals when out jogging, for they are just as wary of my approach as I am of their sudden appearance!

Honouring sacred space

As we receive information through our psychic senses it is tempting to move into the role of the rescuer using the knowledge to 'fix' others, believing that this is our gift to humanity. However, despite good intentions, we may be failing to fulfil our *service* contract, for to enter the sacred space of another without permission is against Universal Law.

Being told: *'There is a dark area over your heart'*, *'You look tired'* or *'I'm sending you healing; I think you need it'* does very little to raise the morale of the receiver and can only benefit the ego of the person who supplies the information and their need to be in control. Similarly, to abdicate responsibility for one's thoughts by saying: *'I'm just relaying what my guides tell me but I don't know really what it means'* or *'I see lots of colours around you. Do you know anything about colours?'* strongly suggests the desire to play power games not only with the client but also with the spirit world.

To blurt out any knowledge which has been received psychically without consideration is not in line with intuitive wisdom, for it is only through detached compassion that we learn how to manage the information which we receive, knowing when to speak and when to stay silent.

As a small child I was aware of being able to read the intention of those I met and sense the state of their subtle energies. This later became useful in my work but embarrassing in new relationships where I found the *'getting to know someone'* period unnecessary and was often accused of never giving anybody a chance. On other occasions, my ability to read someone's inner thoughts left the other person feeling invaded and so, whilst I was experiencing a wonderful feeling of closeness, they erected barriers.

Thankfully, these lessons taught me to respect the sacred space of another and I tend to switch off my intuitive receiver unless I am working, determined to be totally present in the moment rather than observing and analysing the situation from a distance.

Remote viewing

My final thoughts on the subject of psychic powers revolve around the increasing interest in remote viewing, which is clairvoyance practised under strict and scientific guidelines and was originally developed partly out of a scientific interest in psychic matters and partly as a means of heightening National Intelligence. The research has fulfilled its potential by offering us greater insights into the process of consciousness whilst awakening others to their own inner talents.

However, as this practice is now reaching a much wider field, including the business world, I believe that the question which must be asked is: *'What is the purpose or intention behind the action?'*

The spiritual purpose of remote viewing and clairvoyance is to show us that we can communicate telepathically and that our mind is not limited to our three-dimensional world. Any resulting positive expansion of consciousness will always be met by its polar force which can be misused. I suggest that those who are teaching this skill ask themselves: *'Who does this serve; Universal Energy or the individual?'*

Psychic awareness is an essential part of the journey but not the goal. It offers tools which when applied to their best advantage greatly benefit the skills required to live life intuitively. So in essence:

If the psychic powers are the notes, the intuition is the music

Expansion of conciousness: talking with our guides

As the process of transformation continues, the practice of meditation helps to keep us in mind of our soul intent, creating the space where wisdom increases and compassion deepens to sustain us.

We all have guides and loved ones who are supporting us along our journey and it is often in the quiet moments of meditation that the veil thins between the dimensions and we can make contact with them. These beings of Light come from many different sources and include:

1 Our own Guardian angel who remains with us throughout our earth-journey. It is comforting to know that we are never alone and that this loving guidance is always available to us; send out a thought and it will be heard.

2 Individuals who have passed to the other side with whom we were connected, often closely, on this earth especially a partner, parent, grandparent or favourite aunt or uncle.

3 Those in the spirit world from our soul family, whom we may never meet in physical form during this life.

4 Beings from the *deva* and nature kingdoms with whom some people have a natural affinity.

5 Masters, Archangels, Angels and Initiates whose vibrational energy radiates forth and links us to their Greater purpose.

Our soul vibrates at a specific frequency which sets the tone for the quality and purpose of our life experience. This means that we will resonate at the deepest level with all beings of consciousness, whatever their status, who vibrate with the same frequency. This special connection between ourselves and the spirit world means that we can personally experience the powerful wings of an angelic being, the wisdom of an Archangel and the heart beat of a Master.

In the physical world this link leads to a situation where we can make an almost instant connection with someone we have just met and yet spend a lifetime trying to get to know some members of our family!

The presence of individuals from our soul family in our life is often sweet and familiar, based on the fact that we will have been together so many times before. We have been lovers, parents, siblings, friends and teachers, and on many occasions have acted as spirit guides to each other providing the benefit of an overview.

Whatever role we take, we work as a team, with those in the non-material world just as dependent on our actions for their expansion in consciousness as we are for their guidance. Indeed it is worth remembering that while our ancestors guide us, our gift to them is to take on the work which they did not have the time or ability to finish. In accepting this task, we are completing family karma and releasing the souls on all levels to continue their journey without being hampered by unnecessary baggage.

Those who come from the Light will usually present themselves in a form which we find universally acceptable. Therefore many people have guides from the Native American culture, from religious orders, from the Egyptian civilisation, from the Orient and from other indigenous races of this earth. It is their light, love and wisdom we seek and it is not always important to have a name or visual image of the guides who are working with you.

After speaking in public, I am often told of two guides who have been present during my talk, a nun and a Chinese gentleman. I am usually aware of their presence due to the subject matter which is channelled through me, often finding the subtle humour of the Oriental gentleman a great gift and relief when attempting to explain complex esoteric matters.

As we expand our consciousness, the frequencies of our energy bodies accelerate and we become aware of the new levels of communication which are now available to us. This is commonly a time when there is a transfer of responsibility from one guide to another and we value the change in the quality of information which now enters our field of consciousness.

I often imagine that at times when I am particularly slow in appreciating the larger picture, or when I dither over making a decision or disappear into a fog of immaterial concerns, my guides hold an emergency meeting and put me up for auction to the highest bidder!

I know that this would never happen but the thought makes me chuckle and strengthens the bond between us.

A common question I am asked is: *'how do I know whether I'm in contact with a guide or just listening to a part of myself?'* The answer is that, as long as you ask that the guidance comes *from the Light* and with the *desire to do no harm*, then whatever the source the message will always be in harmony with your soul essence. However, I will say that the guidance I receive from the spirit world is often beyond my own life experiences and I am eternally grateful for their overview.

Despite a very close relationship, the spirit world cannot override our free will without affecting their own karma. Therefore, although able to transmit advice and encouragement through the channel of intuition, they cannot carry us and can only stand by and watch if we chose to focus on the glamour or temptations of the denser astral and material worlds.

Most parents would recognise this dilemma as they watch their children enter situations which from the outset look disastrous. However, in retrospect we would all acknowledge that sometimes it is necessary to work through these experiences on our own in order to become stronger and more compassionate towards ourselves and others.

As we grow older we learn the value of listening to the wisdom of experience although there will always be those whose pride prevents them from ever asking for help, making their journey long and laborious.

On many occasions we only request assistance at times of crisis often through the power of prayer and yet the guides are always there for us.

All we need to do is ask!

Of course this doesn't mean that our needs will always be met but we learn that when we are desperate we let go of our expectations around a particular result and miracles happen. Waiting until the last moment when everything else has failed is one way of proceeding along the path; an easier method is to make space for meditation and prayer on a daily basis which helps to develop a healthy channel for invaluable communication and support.

At other times we may feel that we have been abandoned and are unable to understand that if there is a God how could such suffering be allowed and why our guardian angel appears to desert us at times of trouble. I was given this analogy to provide some appreciation of the situation.

Analogy: I was shown a sick child being comforted by its parents whose natural desire was to alleviate the suffering and who were only to happy to take the pain upon themselves. Yet they knew that this was not possible and that it might be necessary to admit the child to hospital to undergo further tests or even an operation which could lead to more distress.

The young child finds it hard to grasp the fact that more pain can lead to comfort and can't understand why people, who profess to love them, refuse to take them away from the source of their anguish. The parents can only stand by offering love, unfailing support and reassurance that things will get better, knowing that the trust which has been built up over the years will be the most crucial factor in this whole episode.

I believe that those who care for us from the world of spirit feel our pain with the compassion of those parents who watch the sick child, willing us to hold on to the thread of hope which will guide us back to the state of wholeness. It is only when we can view our life from the soul's perspective that we can begin to comprehend our earthly passage and understand that where there is love, there is hope.

When we believe that we are loved and feel that love for ourselves then every situation offers the chance to embrace our soul essence and makes emotions such as guilt, fear, hopelessness, shame and self-criticism, obsolete.

The spirit world is essential to human life and has already an intrinsic, yet subtle, relationship with many areas of society including politics, religion, teaching, healing and space exploration. Acceptance of its presence will become more evident in the next few years as we realise that we are not alone and much of what is seen on our planet is purely a reflection of similar occurrences on different strata of existence.

In my working life, I often sense the spirit world as colours and images surrounding those in need and I know that my mind and hands are being guided so as to offer the greatest benefit. If all practitioners could honour and accept their silent helpers and enlist their help, healing would become far more effective and naturally extend to the level of the soul.

A final word of warning, if 'Uncle Joe' lacked common sense on the earth plane remember that dying does not automatically confer him with wings and wisdom. People don't change that quickly! Don't limit yourself; go for gold, asking to be linked to those who represent your very highest aspirations.

I know that my family and close friends help me from the other side but recognise that they are just a small part of a far larger family which overshadows my thoughts, words and actions and works from the Light. Trust which has built up through uncompromising love, sound advice and a joyous sense of humour has created a wonderful bond which guides and supports my work, personal life and Universal service.

Meditation: meeting your guides

Make yourself comfortable and close your eyes.

Imagine yourself on a path.

Become aware of the scenery around you; the colours, smells, sounds and the feel of the wind or sun on your skin and the ground under your feet.

What is the path made from? Sand? Soil? Grass?

What is to either side of the path?

What can you see ahead?

You have with you a bag which can of be any size.

Open the bag and remove from it those things which you choose not to take with you on the next stage of the journey. These may include emotions, limiting beliefs, empty relationships or redundant objects.

If you could add one thing to the bag, do so now.

When you are ready, pick up the bag and walk forward along the path.

Allow your senses to appreciate the changing scenery as you progress.

Now coming towards you is someone from the spirit world who loves you dearly.

It may be someone whom you have known on the earth plane or someone whom you recognise as a spirit guide.

You greet each other and you are enfolded in their unconditional love
for you.

It may be appropriate to ask them a question at this time; ask your
question and listen for the reply.

Walk a little way with them, remembering the special place they occupy
in your life.

Now it is time for them to leave and they remind you that they will
always be present for you on some level.

Before they leave they give you a gift to help you on your way. Receive
the gift.

You may wish to give something in return. Give your gift.

Make your farewells and watch as they walk away, leaving you standing
on the path, with your feelings, thoughts and gift.

*In your own time, slowly bring your awareness back into the room;
become aware of your hands and feet, your breathing and, when you
are ready, open your eyes.*

*This exercise can be repeated whenever you feel alone, confused
or just need to be encircled within that wonderful embrace of love.*

5 Thought liberation: clearing a path through the mind

A moment's insight is sometimes worth a life's experience

Oliver Wendell Holmes, *The Professor at the Breakfast Table,* **1809–1894**

The next stage of the journey requires us to clear a path through the myriad of thoughtforms which have been produced over the years and decide which ones to keep and which to discard. It is easy for our mind to resemble an attic filled with beliefs and aspirations which have at one time had a place in our life. But they now clutter up this lofty space due to our tendency to hoard, either through sentimentality or with the conviction that one day we will find a use for these neglected concepts.

Thoughtforms are created by the increasingly important mental body which focuses and structures those aspects of our life which will bring soul development, contribution and harmony. Unfortunately many of our personal problems arise from an unwillingness to relinquish thoughtforms which no longer serve us or to use them as a means of avoiding change and often, paradoxically, reaching our full soul potential and ultimate happiness.

Thoughts take three forms, all of which are extremely valuable and which reflect mankind's place as co-creator within this world of matter. They can be described as:

1 **Those which are acquired, learned or passed down through the generations** often as rules, mottoes or beliefs, providing structure and meaning to the world we inhabit and without which there

would be chaos. Some of these thoughtforms are the result of previous personal experience, family codes and social ethics whilst others emerge from global institutions such as science, philosophy, politics, education and religion.

2 Those which are created to bring reason and stability to an experience where the emotional component has the potential to overwhelm. These thoughtforms allow us to rise above the swirling waters of our emotional or desire body, preventing us from drowning in our feelings and unconsciously reacting to every situation which appears as a threat.

3 Those which surround an idea which, although inspirational, is relatively nebulous and requires focus in order to become manifest. It is the intuition which oversees this process, enlisting the help of the logic and emotions to bring spirit into matter in accordance with the Greater Plan.

 ## Our thoughts create our perception of reality

It is well-known that *energy follows thought* yet most people are still surprised when someone who has been on their mind suddenly telephones or when something we imagined would happen, transpires. As we enter the Aquarian Age it is vitally important that we accept our role as co-creator in this world, appreciating that this will inevitably include those things of which we are proud as well as episodes we would rather forget!

In scientific terms, it is seen that within the solid, molecular world, the gravitational force of the Earth plays an important role in determining the rate and direction of movement of any particular object. However, at the sub-atomic level, details are far less easy to define with gravity exerting a minimal effect. Here we see Heisenberg's Principle of Uncertainty in action showing that the movement of particles such as protons, neutrons etc. cannot be accurately established

without considering the influence of other electro-magnetic forces which **must** include the electrical impulses of the mind.

Therefore, as our consciousness expands beyond the limited confines of the material world and encompasses the higher vibrational forces of logic and intuition, our thoughts increasingly play a major role in the creation of our reality.

With this in mind, it shows us how important it is to be aware of our thoughts and to reject those which no longer serve our soul purpose or the common good. This process of selection requires us to understand the three levels of thoughtform creation, which will now be discussed in greater detail.

Learned thoughtforms

*Knowledge dwells in heads replete with thoughts of
other men; wisdom in minds attentive to their own.*
William Cooper, *The Task*

These acquired beliefs have usually been developed and gathered over many generations and passed down via various mediums such as the spoken word, poetry, song, dance, art and the written word. Their actual origin has often been lost in the mists of time and yet, for those individuals who are still relatively unconscious and who slumber under tribal law, these thoughtforms represent the major blueprint on which their life is structured.

The brain stores beliefs about most things, and these are expressed in terms of individual and global concerns:

- *'I believe/know/feel that . . . '* (Individual belief)
- *'The world is/life is/children should . . . '* (Global belief)

Many of these mottoes or perceptions of ourselves just slip off the tongue and below I include a few common phrases I have heard whilst teaching and ask you to notice what comes to mind when you review your own personal beliefs associated with the following themes:

- Self: . . . 'Who are you?'
      'I am married, have three children and work in an
      office'
  (It is easy to bury our sense of self beneath our identity in the
  world . . . 'Who *are you?*'
- Love: . . . '*I feel loved when people like me*'
  (This demands much from the world where inevitably there will
  be some who feel indifferent towards you!)
- Relationships, partners and friends: . . . '*Friends stand by you
  through thick and thin*'
- Families including children and parents: . . . '*Keep it in the
  family; don't let anybody outside the family know our business*'
- Health and illness: . . . '*Health is peace of mind*'
- Money: . . . '*Money doesn't grow on trees*'
- Looks and body image: . . . '*You're only as old as you feel*'
- Work: . . . '*Work, work, work and when you finish working,
  work!*'
  (Relayed to me during a visit to a post-Communist country)

I am in no doubt as to the power of these thoughts, recognising
scenarios from my own life and from that of others, which are created
time and again in response to a long held belief. In my classes on
Mind/Body medicine I ask participants to remember what happened
when they were ill in childhood and also to look back at the effect of
illnesses in relatives who shared the same home.

In the Western World, 70% of the audience will tell me that they
received more attention and nurturing when sick than they did when
well. Although perfectly understandable, it also highlights an important
factor behind the emergence of ill health and one which I do not believe
is being addressed in Health Care programmes.

My assertion is not that people are malingering but rather that
many learn that it is often only through illness that they receive the love
and support which should be granted without having to play *Russian
Roulette* with one's physical body. Only through honest communication, the willingness to give without conditions and the skills to
nurture oneself, will deep healing result.

As a side line, a number of the participants questioned reported being told to *'exercise mind over matter'* and to *'keep going'*. Now, in their adult life, these individuals have a marked tendency to either still disregard any illness, often to their own detriment, or to take time off work at the slightest sign of a cold. Mind control and denial are powerful coping mechanisms but can be inappropriate when the life force of the individual is unable to overcome the state of disease without external intervention.

Our intellect creates beliefs with the positive intention of providing us with guidance, signposts and warnings so as to make our journey as smooth as possible. However, it is important to review our mental baggage periodically and relinquish that which no longer serves present day circumstances.

The intuition's role in this *spring cleaning* session is to create scenarios which challenge our patterns of thought and use our feelings as reliable indicators of the degree of resonance between the belief and our soul essence. Therefore when we feel frustrated, restricted or depressed by a situation it is usually an underlying belief which needs to change in order to allow us to flow once again with the river of life.

However, there are times when we prefer our own version of the truth, refusing to see the danger signs which are so obvious to everybody else and need a crisis or an outpouring of unconditional love to stop us in our tracks.

Another important step is to become aware of the sequence of thoughts behind one's actions and ask whether they are still relevant.

A Legend

A newly married wife is preparing to cook a ham for a family meal. As she places the ham in a pan, her husband exclaims:

'You can't cook a ham like that; you have to cut it in half and
cook it in two pans'.
'Why?' asks the young woman, adding: 'Who told you that?'
'My mother'. So they go to see the mother. 'How do you cook a
ham?'
'You cut it in half and place it in two pans', replies the mother.
'Who told you that?' ask the couple in unison. 'Your
grandmother', replies the mother.
So they go to see the grandmother. 'How do you cook a ham?'
'Well you divide it in half and cook it in two pans', answers the
old woman.
'Why?' they all demand. And the grandmother replies with
the very simple answer: 'Because I only have two small
pans!'

Logic and reason are built on practicality and experience but we
sometimes need to reassess our beliefs and move with the times!

Much learned knowledge is taught parrot fashion and without
question, with the unspoken understanding that any challenge could
cause serious instability to the basic structure of families, countries,
cultures or even the planet. This is certainly apparent during govern-
mental discussions concerning the possible existence of life on other
planets and whether there has been any communication with UFOs.
There is now increasing evidence to show that much information has
been suppressed although the 'authorities' insist that they are only trying
to prevent public panic.

This rather curious belief that UFOs would be greeted with fear
makes me wonder why it is necessary to create an *external enemy* and
suggests that a more harmonious meeting could threaten those who
govern our lives at present.

I think the paternalistic approach of the rule makers does not
always take into account the increasing accessibility of vast amounts of
information to anybody with the right receiver, via systems such as the
Internet and extensive media coverage. We will always require a certain
degree of regulation through the development of laws and statutes. But
this should be designed through a consensus which honours and

respects the wisdom of all souls on this planet whatever their age, race or gender and which encourages individual responsibility.

Information is reaching us from many levels, demanding an expansion in consciousness in line with Universal thinking. It is part of the intuitive journey not only to discard unnecessary or invalid thoughts but also to be sufficiently mentally flexible to integrate facts which bring greater understanding to our existence.

As a medical student, I was taught like many others before me (and after) that the pain of angina radiates from the heart down the left arm and into the fingers. Despite knowing that the nerve supply to the fingers and the heart are different, I was happy to accept this anomaly from the lips of my revered professors. That was until I started to teach!

Becoming a teacher really brings you down to earth quickly, highlighting the limits of your knowledge.

'*If the nerve supply is different, why does the pain travel down the arm?*' asks the fervent student who is hanging on your every word, while you are trying desperately to brush over the subject.

It wasn't until I studied the meridians or energy lines of Oriental Medicine that the conundrum was solved. I discovered that it was the heart meridian which made the connection, extending from the heart down the arm to the little finger. At last I could stand in front of the class with a valid answer!

So much of orthodox medicine has no rational explanation and yet so many of my own profession are unwilling to broaden their awareness to include subjects which they see as illogical!

One man's myth is another man's reason

Reason is itself a matter of faith. It is an act of faith to assert that our thoughts have any relation to reality at all.
G.K. Chesterton, *Orthodoxy*, 1874–1936

The dictionary describes a myth as '*A purely fictitious narrative usually involving supernatural characters and embodying popular beliefs on natural phenomena'*. With an open mind it is clear to see that all cultures encompass a degree of mythology, some of which is more visible than others, depending on the society.

But someone's myth is another person's reason. It is purely a matter of perspective and it is arrogant and naive to ridicule the beliefs of others without first examining one's own logic.

Our knowledge of this Earth's history is extremely limited and often dependent on the reasoning and consciousness of the archaeologists and scientists of the day. Without intuitive awareness these experts purely synthesise what has been discovered with previous knowledge and create a myth which is then taught in our schools.

However, many of these assumptions are being disputed by people who have taken what they have discovered and applied it to a much larger picture. Hence in Central America and Egypt they have produced totally different theories, suggesting that there were highly developed civilisations 12,000 years ago which appear to have evolved from cultures whose origins stretch back over 100,000 years. This new evidence discredits the view that man was primitive until approximately 4000 BC.

My vision is that over the next 15 years history, geography and science textbooks will need to be rewritten to encompass new and exciting discoveries. However, I also believe that we could not have reached this point earlier due to our limited mental abilities and to the fact that there is a right time for everything.

I have been shown that the spirit world has the ability to hold certain *objects* within the 4th, 5th and even 6th dimensions out of reach of our three-dimensional visual field and that when it is important for a major shift in human consciousness to occur, these objects take on a physical form and are *discovered*.

Every story or myth has a truth somewhere in time.

There are certain cultures where myths concerning the supernatural world are part of the normal fabric of law-making. This is true in Ireland where many people have a *fairy ring* on their land which usually consists of a circle of trees where it is believed the fairies play. No Irish man or woman would ever consider cutting down those trees and building on that site; consequently, roads take some interesting turns, all to avoid this sacred ring.

Any foreigner who has disregarded this common law has met with one disaster after another and has eventually abandoned their project. What lies behind the myth is unclear but I suspect that it is strongly connected to the preservation of earth energies essential for the abundance of the land.

Myths like this represent a collective thoughtform which has tremendous power and plays an important role in situations such as the placebo effect, faith healing, team support and prayer. As we will see in the next chapter, it is inherent in those who cultivate the myth to take responsibility for the effect of its manifestation.

In the field of global medicine, I have been privileged to watch shamans produce sand paintings which represent the state of health of an individual at that time. By carefully moving specific grains of sand, he/she attempts to change the flow of energy through the patient and hence generate a cure.

A similar procedure carried out in Japan asks the patient to create a flower arrangement which expresses their health using their intuition rather than their intellect. Certain stems are then removed or relocated by the healer in order to bring about healing.

Such healing rituals differ from those of Western cultures by placing the individual in the centre of a global picture reminding him or her of the interconnected nature of all life forms, whilst also assisting them towards a central role in their own life. I perceive that true health cannot be achieved, even when physical well being is restored, while the spirit resides on the periphery of human consciousness.

A final word on this subject comes from my experiences in the hospital in New Zealand where the main patient population was Maori. One of their beliefs was that if a bird flew through the windows of a house, someone in that house would die. The weather was hot and sultry that particular summer and the windows were wide open. I can still remember the challenge a small sparrow presented to modern medicine as it gaily flew up and down the ward followed by a team of screaming Europeans determined to help its passage to the outside world, watched in amazement by patients and visitors who probably believed that this was part of our particular healing ritual!

A sceptic may say that all these beliefs are pure *faith healing* where the confidence in the technique or healer is the most important part of the cure. I would totally agree, accepting the power of the mind to heal, but would question whether modern medicine does not also rely heavily on the patient's expectations and faith in the doctor, reinforced by shrewd advertising.

Logic and scepticism

I thoroughly enjoy discussions with healthy sceptics who have open inquiring minds but have little time for those who cling to their standard questions and responses without ever being willing to consider another position.

Whilst honouring the role of fixed thoughtforms, I suggest that we all look at those beliefs which we cling to with such tenacity and devotion that we suffocate the creative spark and recognise the fear of the unknown which commonly lurks behind a sceptical point of view. Let us begin to employ research not to prove what we already know or in the desire to disapprove someone else's theory but to use what we know as a starting point to expand our knowledge base and hence our level of consciousness.

Emotions attracting thoughtforms

Even though the mental function of the human race is developing fast our feelings still play a powerful, often subconscious, role in directing many of our daily activities. On experiencing any emotion, whether positive or negative, we surround this discharge with a thoughtform which subdues the unpleasant fluctuations of the desire body and provides meaning to life situations. In other words, we create a belief which makes life more manageable.

'I feel this way because . . . '

The formation of this belief often resonates with something we already know about ourselves acquired through earlier experiences or past life episodes.

'I know this is true as it has happened to me before'

However, in our desire to find meaning in the unsettling world of emotions, we can construct a rationale which to an observer appears completely irrational. This response needs to be distinguished from an intuitive insight, where there may be also no logical sequence of thoughts leading to the conclusion, but here the emotional involvement is practically insignificant.

Stimulation of the energy centres is also very different, with the Heart chakra being activated in the case of intuition, whereas emotions tend to centre around the Solar plexus, situated in the upper abdomen leading to gut feelings.

Analogy: You go for an interview and fail to be offered the job despite an excellent CV and having given what you believe to be, a good performance. In the aftermath, you silently berate the interviewing panel for not recognising true talent and then convince yourself that you were too good for the job and wouldn't take it even if they got down on their hands and knees and begged you.

However, the less confident part of you which is feeling the pain of rejection starts to search for reasons based on previous experience and programming.

'It's my appearance. They just didn't like the way I looked.
It's because of my big nose. Maybe if I had surgery, I would be
accepted'.

(In reality, they had already chosen someone in-house and hence the interview was purely a technicality).

In this way we create *thought bubbles* which extend further and further from the truth and from the offending emotion. Instead of dealing with the core of the problem we devote time and money to a project which will probably have minimal effect and simply postpones the moment when we need to face reality. Of course, there will always be practitioners who are only too happy to liberate some of our money and fix the hapless nose without attempting to discover the true cause of distress!

There is much scientific evidence to suggest that long term suppression of emotions plays an important role in the formation of the dis-ease state. These emotions are often cloaked in a belief which suggests resolution and that everything is FINE, while the emotions quietly fester underneath.

While this trapped emotional energy exists, it transforms the surrounding thought or belief into a powerful signal which when transmitted will have a major impact on the creation of our future story.

Analogy: A young woman believes that she is unlovable and constantly demands reassurance from those around her. This becomes very wearing on her friends and eventually they drift away. With a sigh of resignation she says:

'I am unlovable.'

One day she meets a wonderful man who adores her. Since this reality is not in accord with her own inner belief she does everything in her power to drive him away, including accusing him of infidelity. When he can stand it no longer, he leaves and through her tears she says with a hint of triumph:

'I told you so. I am unlovable!'

Unfortunately, many people waste their energy re-creating episodes which add nothing to their soul growth and fail to contribute to global efforts, believing that they are powerless to change the situation. Yet, in truth, there are many steps which can be taken to transform a belief into something which is constructive rather than destructive. This may require professional advice and support such as provided by a psychotherapist or psychologist.

Positive Steps include:

1 **Recognising persistent patterns in your life by reflecting on major events in the past:**
- What is the subconscious message or belief which keeps recurring?
- Is there a particular manner in which you respond to challenging situations?
- Have you discovered in retrospect what you needed to learn from the event or, in other words, how did you change because of the episode?

2 **Accessing the emotions:**
- Recognising that there will be times when emotions need to be expressed openly and that, when this is performed in a loving and non-judgemental manner, *'I feel . . . etc.'*, the reaction of others is not your concern.
- Writing a letter you never send, burning it afterwards to release the energy.
- Keeping a journal of thoughts and feelings.
- Speaking to someone who will listen without judgement or without their need to *'fix'* you.
- Painting, drawing or sculpting your feelings and continuing until there is resolution.

3 **Choosing new ways to respond such as:**
- Counting to ten.
- Taking three deep breaths allowing longer on the out breath.

- Changing your posture by, for instance, lifting up your head, uncrossing your hands, straightening your spine or slightly bending your knees to lower the centre of gravity and become more stable.
- Smiling at yourself and letting this extend to all those you meet.

4 Being honest when you ask yourself: *'How am I benefiting by holding onto this belief or by continually behaving in this manner?'*

- Does the reinforcement of this belief about myself provide me with an odd sense of security?
- Am I acting in defiance of the expectations of others? Am I being a rebel despite the discomfort the situation creates?
- Do I receive what I need in terms of nurturing, love, support and encouragement only by maintaining my stand?
- Who would I be and how would I act if I let go of this belief about myself and others?
- What would be expected of me if I took on my own power and stopped hiding behind false beliefs?

When we do face the powerful *dragon* of unexpressed emotions, we find it contains the energy essential for soul transformation, delivering us safely from a lifetime of restriction and lack of true purpose.

Karma

Karma or the Universal Law of Cause and Effect expresses the concept that *'As you sow, so will you reap'*. This can be interpreted to include: *'Do unto others as you wish to be done unto you'* or *'That which you believe, you will perceive to occur'*.

Karma influences us on many levels, affecting the individual, families, cultures and the planet's evolution. Man's understanding of its control on our life has produced some interesting results:

1 We express a notion or belief which dutifully follows karmic law and becomes manifest and still we exclaim somewhat in surprise:

'I knew that would happen; it always does!'.

2 We blame karma for a doomed life, never attempting to push out the boundaries or plant new seeds, often fearful that either option would inevitably demand attention:

'It's my karma to suffer' (but not silently!)

3 We attempt to clean our karmic slate by carrying out noble deeds which, hopefully, do not accrue new karma. However, our need to inform everybody of our act, or the smug feeling of self-satisfaction, immediately defeats the object.

4 We like to imagine that the suffering we are experiencing is as a consequence of being a victim in past lives and hence now it is time for us to receive in abundance. It is interesting to note, however, that most people fail to recall the lives when they were the aggressor or power crazy and that perhaps karma is now offering them the opportunity to appreciate the other side of the coin. Selective memory can be very useful!

5 *Instant karma* shows that time is irrelevant on the other dimensions.

'I was just telling my friends how I worry about not having enough money when I leave this job and almost the next minute I find that my purse has been stolen and I have to find my way home by asking strangers for help. Talk about instant karma!'

Be careful when you challenge the Universe; it has plenty of tricks up its sleeve to help us to move beyond our fears and into our power!

When the creation of thoughtforms is a conscious decision we become masters of cause and effect with an increasing ability to appreciate our role in the Greater Plan. Karma will still have an effect but we become proactive in our life and are no longer drawn into addictive emotional games, the acquisition of material wealth for status or the hoarding of out-of-date thoughtforms for security.

So, by listening to the still small voice of our intuition, we can progressively pull away from the powerful hold that karma has on our lives and become conscious participants in the creative process.

Thoughtform to focus inspiration

When we receive an inspirational idea it is often unstructured and requires focus, vitality and form in order for it to become active on this Earth. It is the role of the intuition to direct the creative spark through the logic and emotions and provide it with a physical identity so that it can achieve optimal effect.

In this way, the intuitive thoughtform accelerates the progress of an idea towards manifestation, which is very different from the other types of thoughtform which usually limit flow by applying strict conditions to the acceptance of this flash of inspiration.

Alice Bailey says: *'Don't fit the truth into the hour, but the hour into the truth'*.

By clearing a way through the many thoughtforms which move in and out of our consciousness and becoming mindful of creating thoughts which reflect the harmony, wisdom and compassion of our soul, we offer ourselves as worthy channels for the Breath of God.

Truth

*Truth is a pathless land, and you cannot approach it
by any path whatsoever, by any religion, by any sect.*

Jiddu Krishnamurti, from a speech in 1931

To complete this chapter, I would like to bring together the different
thoughtforms under the banner of truth. Truth is often spoken of in
terms of providing a definitive response and yet it is multi-dimensional
and dependent on so many different factors.

Truth can relate to:

1 Learned knowledge and personal experiences.

2 Knowledge in respect of an emotional reaction.

3 Intuitive insight.

Perhaps the best we can do is to be honest and tell the truth as we
know it, honouring the truth that belongs to others.

Exercise to accelerate the flow of intuitive thoughtforms

Take a piece of paper (A4 size) or open your journal.

Make yourself comfortable.

With a pen or pencil write no more than 8 words in the centre of the
paper relating to an idea which has been at the back of your mind for

sometime or perhaps a notion which entered your thoughts through a dream or meditation.

Using the flowing energy of the intuition, create a *mind map* where you produce radiating lines like the *spokes* of a wheel. Write at the end of the lines everything which relates to bringing this idea into manifestation. Some of the *thoughts* may have sub-sections; let it flow.

e.g.

Try not to stop and think but allow the pen/pencil to guide you.

Don't limit the opportunities available to you.

Allow the end to arrive naturally and acknowledge that the original thought may have opened a passageway to a very interesting conclusion which reveals a *longing* which has been buried inside for far too long. Once the awareness has been realised, the initial idea can be released.

Become quiet and ask inside that your thoughts will be heard and become manifest if it is the Will of the Creator. Thank your inner guidance for its support and the Universe for the forthcoming response.

It is now time to put into action the thoughts on the mind map, starting with those which are most practical and then wait.

Every week check to see how far this idea is progressing, being prepared to abandon this inspiration when, as a result of your activities, another idea takes priority.

Don't get despondent when things seem to take a long time or perhaps things don't work out as you wished.

Check that your old *acquired thoughtforms* or *emotionally based thoughtforms* are not undermining your efforts.

Keep the channel clear. Know your prayers have been heard and believe that there is a time and place for everything.

Have fun and remember: it's a mental world; what we believe happens!

6 Harnessing the will: the power to direct energy

Where love rules, there is no will to power, and where power predominates, love is lacking. The one is the shadow of the other.

Carl Justav Jung, *Gesammelte Werke vol. 7*, **1917**

As we begin the next stage of our pilgrimage, we reflect on the tremendous transformation which has occurred since we set forth on our quest. Through the gentle urgings of the intuition we have reclaimed our personal power, walked through the emotional mists of illusion and left behind many of the myopic perceptions which we held about ourselves and others.

We are lighter in spirit, mind and body with the atoms of our being now vibrating at far higher frequencies. Without much effort changes have also taken place in our dietary habits, exercise requirements, sleep patterns and the practice of meditation; certain things (and even people) have become redundant whilst space has become naturally available for new experiences.

At last we feel free and in charge of our life sensing that anything is possible and excited by the innumerable opportunities waiting to engage our attention and energy. Yet, in this mental world, this section of the journey is probably one of the most challenging for with the acquisition of power comes the responsibility to use it wisely. Such wisdom can be only partially taught due to the fickle nature of mankind, leaving the remainder to emerge from an inner sense of personal morality which is accessed primarily through the intuition.

Compared with emotional game playing which is relatively unconscious, the manipulation of other people which can occur at this level is far more powerful and potentially destructive because it involves the will of the individual which implies full awareness of the situation. When the will is driven by the desire to work for the greater good and not by the need to boost one's own personal ego then the outcome will be positive.

However, since we know that energy follows thought there will always be a response whether the motive is humanitarian or not and who amongst us can be the final arbiter when deciding what is best for mankind, for the nature kingdoms and for Universal well-being.

History reminds us that many people, among them kings, generals and spiritual leaders, believed they knew the truth and asked others to follow them, often to their death. It is not for us to judge *their* actions in retrospect but to learn from their example and to question the ethics which lie behind the decisions and goals which demand our attention at this time.

The challenge for the individual is to align their will to the pure, clear note which sounds forth from the depth of their soul and which is in harmony with the Eternal Will. This requires mindfulness and a willingness to avoid the glamour and other temptations which are so seductive at this stage of the journey.

One's *motive* or *intention* is the key in this endeavour and needs to be studied carefully from an objective viewpoint for it is easy to become lost in the belief that we act for the benefit of planetary consciousness whilst secretly lining our own egotistical pockets.

It is good to remember that intuition serves three purposes:

1 It encourages the *soul to grow* and reach its full potential.

2 It brings *greater awareness* to the individual which, in turn, increases collective consciousness.

3 It *benefits the Universe* more than the individual with such service starting at home.

Intuition does not:

1 Purely satisfy our trivial personal needs.

2 Mean that we will never suffer or be in pain but hopefully this will be short-lived.

3 Lead to personal gain at the expense of others.

4 Deny the need for confrontation.

5 Always lead to action; stillness is a gift.

6 Necessarily lead to separation but often to greater commitment especially to the family and the community

7 Eradicate the need for self-examination which may indeed become heightened.

As we flex our energetic muscles and consciously become aware of our ability to shape our reality we encounter several phenomena which, although appearing miraculous at first, are all part of learning to direct energy with pure intent.

Manifestation

One God, one law, one element
And one far-off divine event,
To which the whole creation moves.
Alfred, Lord Tennyson, *In Memoriam,* **1850**

Our whole existence is based on our ability to bring Spirit into matter, to make the invisible, visible, and to bring nebulous ideas into reality. Therefore, manifestation or materialisation is not a new concept or one just pertinent to the end of the 20th Century. What is changing is our perception of our part in this creative process and how we can create a life which reflects our spiritual blueprint.

Manifestation relies on changing the vibrational frequency of the energy within particles, sound and light in order to create a new form of existence. It is dependent on a sense of direction and a source of power, hence:

MANIFESTATION = INTENTION + POWER

Throughout this pilgrimage we have encountered various types of power and intention and it is now time to study the effect of our will upon our world. First, however, I want to outline the process so far, giving examples where appropriate:

Basic manifestation

Despite the heading there is nothing crude about this level of creation for it involves almost all aspects of our existence, most of which we take for granted. The endless discussion between those who believe in Creation versus those who believe in Evolution has failed to resolve: *'Who or what is the great designer behind this breathtaking display called life?'*

Not wishing to take this debate any further, I see mankind's role in the scheme as not inconsequential for every thought, word and action is an essential ingredient in the creative process.

Manifestation through emotion

When the **intention** is **desire** and the **power** is **emotion**, manifestation occurs mainly subconsciously. Hence, *we inwardly want something* and apply the energy of our emotions (fear, anger, passion, despair and happiness) to achieve the required change in frequency in order to summon the object of our desire into form.

But as the well-known saying states: *'Be careful what you ask for, you might just get it!'*

Fear attracts fear and anger attracts anger even when they are not outwardly expressed. Without conscious awareness we can become victims of our own creation as well as failing to learn to take responsibility for their effect on our inner and outer worlds.

Strong emotions can often result in an immediate and surprising outcome as seen in the following examples:

A Vehicle of Emotions   Our car usually symbolises the means by which our spiritual aspirations, thoughtforms and emotions are transported whilst on this earth plane, hopefully with the soul in charge of the steering wheel and not relegated to the back seat. Therefore, anything which happens to our car is usually a clear reflection of our life at that time.

One day as I was travelling along a motorway, my mind kept wandering over the events of the past few weeks (whilst, of course, I kept my eyes on the road ahead!). A long-term relationship had recently finished and I was feeling extremely vulnerable.

I was reminded of similar emotions in the past when it felt as if the bottom had fallen out of my world and I wasn't sure if I could summon up enough energy to pick myself up and start all over again. I remember letting out a huge sigh of exhaustion and saying 'Not again, God'.

At that exact moment, the engine started to splutter and the car lost power with the only option available being to guide the vehicle onto the hard shoulder. Knowing little about mechanical matters, beyond first aid measures, I waited for help which fortunately arrived fairly quickly.

When the rescue crew looked inside the bonnet, they were amazed to see that one of the sparking plugs had unscrewed itself and was lying on the other side of the engine.

'How did that happen?' they exclaimed and I thought:
'What can I say that they would understand . . . you see, all I did
      was let out a really deep sigh!'

Since then, I have been much more careful where and when I express myself emotionally!

Making Friends with Electrical Equipment   The intimate relationship we have with our car leads on to the next form of manifestation or rather malfunction which is relatively common. How many of you have a love/hate relationship with electrical equipment where you *lower* *your voice* and *speak sweetly* whenever you're in the vicinity of your computer, fax machine, washing machine or toaster?

These machines seem to sense any disturbance in our energy field, working perfectly well until we are in a hurry or somehow out of sorts then all kinds of problems arise which naturally do little for our already ragged state of mind.

Such energy swings are more common in those who are emotionally charged, highly sensitive to atmospheres or poorly grounded energetically. Perhaps there should be a special type of *warranty* provided with the equipment purchased by psychics, spiritual disciples and electrically unstable human beings! How often do we hear that microphones failed to work in lectures, tape recorders didn't record and high quality cameras were unsuccessful in producing a single picture when in the presence of certain individuals.

There is a tendency to say *'It just wasn't meant'* which absolves all those concerned from any form of liability, but these malfunctions are purely reflecting our own impressionable electrical nature.

Computers deserve their own separate mention since they often choose *what should be printed* and *what should be deleted* without consultation with their human owner. Like many people I have been totally frustrated when losing a whole morning's work only later to have to agree with the *edit* function that perhaps it was just as well that I hadn't submitted that section to my publishers!

(You will not be surprised to learn that as I write this chapter, my Internet modem has started to malfunction. The technical adviser whom I contacted asked whether there had been an electrical storm in my area as this sometimes causes a problem. I lamely accepted his explanation even though I know the weather has been fine every day! What could I say: 'Well you see, I'm writing this chapter on . . . ')

The final energetic disturbance which I have seen manifest in my presence is for lights to dim or fail whether this is in a street, a shopping centre or in my own home. I am inclined to associate this with times when I am excited, full of energy or when I feel strongly linked to the spirit world, reminding me that:

First and foremost we are electrical beings.

Ask and you will receive   I wonder how many people have sent out the plea, usually sub-consciously: *'I need more time'* and, almost instantaneously, appointments are cancelled and the time is available. However if, like me in my early days of practice, you lack confidence in your abilities, you will then spend much of this valuable time wondering why the clients failed to attend!

The Universe hears our thoughts and meets our needs but so often we turn away from the open door and search in vain for reasons to reject the gift or berate ourselves for not asking earlier. Gratitude and self-love are the keys which free us from the spider's web of obsessional thoughts and allow us to move forward and enjoy the gifts which are offered.

Manifestation through thoughtforms

We have already explored the different ways in which we build thought-forms so as to create a stable environment in which to live and where the **intention** for manifestation is our **belief system** and the **power** comes from the **emotions**:

'I believe, therefore it is'.

Much of this manifestation is unconscious although we are becoming increasingly aware of our need to change our beliefs in order to change our reality otherwise we find ourselves in a safe but boring rut. Manifestation on this level can reveal hidden thoughtforms and become a highly constructive teacher as shown in the next example:

My body: my friend   Throughout my career in the caring professions, I have been continually impressed by the body's ability to manifest our thoughts with such power and accuracy. **Nothing** appears by chance; everything contains a message and the more our life is disrupted by that event, the greater the need to heed that message.

An example of the mind and body working in harmony occurred when I was preparing a seminar called 'Loving yourself, warts and all'.

The evening before the Workshop, I noticed a large verruca (an inwardly growing wart) on the sole of my foot exactly over the area representing the heart in reflexology.

Knowing that warts represent that part of ourselves which we find difficult to love, I thought what a wonderful example of *walking one's talk*! This amazing messenger allowed me to look at aspects of my being which I found difficult to accept and encouraged me to integrate them into my life with love. And when this had happened, the wart just disappeared.

The final example shows how old beliefs can obstruct the flow of energy used in manifestation even though, outwardly, we may be very eager to achieve a result. This situation is common in those who have had a very formal religious up-bringing and who then attempt to adopt *New Age* thinking. The chasm between believing and knowing can only be bridged by an open heart of trust and by accepting that there is place for all disciplines of life.

Now you see it and now you don't   Last year whilst travelling in Peru I visited Machu Picchu which, snuggled amongst the majestic and all-embracing Andes, was the magical place I had seen in my dreams. The unrelenting rain did little to dampen my enthusiasm and we were blessed with having this sacred site almost to ourselves.

One afternoon, as the grey clouds hung heavily over the mountain tops and the mist enshrouded the valley, three of us decided to direct a little positive prayer towards the darkened skies:

'If it be Thy will, let there be a break in the clouds' we thought in unison and, on opening our eyes, we were thrilled to be able to see the trains making their way along the side of the river, hundreds of feet below us. Encouraged by our own success, we decided to go one stage further:

'If it be Thy will, let the sun shine upon Machu Picchu'. Instantaneously, I felt heat on the top of my head and, on looking, saw the rays of sunlight streaming down upon the sacred site.

At this, my enthusiasm and ego got the better of me and I thought 'I don't believe that happened' and immediately the sun disappeared behind the clouds. Just as suddenly, I received an inner message that said '*Of course the sun appeared; remember energy always follows thought; what stopped the flow was your ego and disbelief*'.

What a lesson! I realised that there were times when there was perfect synastry between my thoughts and my beliefs but at other times my mind said one thing and my heart another, bringing doubt and distortion to the messages I transmitted to the Universe.

The strength which emerges from trusting and following the intuition is powerful and unshakeable and results from every cell of our being working in total harmony leaving no room for confusion.

Manifestation and the will

Now we reach the section of the journey where the **will** becomes the **intention** and the **power** may be the **emotions, the psychic force** or **love**. As stated previously, when the will is involved we are consciously aware of our activities and hence the outcome is far more powerful than that which follows the erratic expression of the subconscious.

> **With consciousness comes responsibility and the need to be clear about our motive or intention.**

All these stages of development are essential as a learning experience but our journey takes us towards a state of manifestation which comes from an open heart and mind, where one's will reflects the will of the whole and where the ego is not the primary consideration.

In our mind, we have moved through hoping and believing and have reached our Shangri-La, that essence of knowing which is not restricted to the brain but exists within every atom of our being and where there is *no attachment* to the knowing.

Let me share with you some of the steps along the way starting with:

The will and the emotions

Synchronicity This type of manifestation has reached cult levels recently with *coincidence* being relegated to the misinformed or to those who wish to believe that life is not completely fated! Synchronicity is defined as *events occurring at the same time* and implies that there is a direct link between all states of existence so that our thoughts and words can lead to almost instantaneous action. Thus we hear phrases such as:

> *'I was just thinking of you when you rang!'*
> *'I knew it would be you!'*
> *'I sat down and guess who should sit next to me?'*
> *'I turned on the television and couldn't believe that they were talking about . . . '.*
> *'Of all the people to meet at the concert after twenty five years; I'd only been talking about them earlier in the day'.*

We are still amazed and impressed by synchronicity even though as New Age thinkers we like to believe that we accept the principle of simultaneous action.

> *'I really shouldn't be surprised but when it happens it sends shivers up my spine!'*

The vibration of thought travels beyond the confines of time and space through a complex etheric network of communication channels which far exceeds anything which modern man has presently developed. It is hard for us not to focus on absolute time which offers a past, a present and a future and yet in our sleep state we are content to step beyond these limits and travel in our dreams backwards and forwards with great ease and then happily awaken into a temporal existence which is linear.

Synchronicity has always existed. What has changed is our conscious appreciation of its occurrence although we are often less willing to acknowledge its role when we are brought face to face with someone whom we were desperately hoping to avoid! Unfortunately, the higher echelons of consciousness are not particularly interested in our likes and dislikes and tend to send everything with the same conviction that *if you think it* then it needs to become manifest.

Like most people, my own life has been full of synchronous events which include:

- Seeing a leaflet in a Healing Centre where I was giving a talk, miles from my home, advertising a course run by someone to whom I had been introduced by a friend the previous week and at the time had thought 'I want to learn more from that person'.

  Now, two years later, I can see why the contact was so important.

- Meeting a stranger in a book shop who told me about the Mayan crystal skull two days after I had received confirmation of a trip to Central America to travel the Maya Ruta (more later).

- Realising that I was sitting next to the person whom I had wanted to meet at a conference but had missed, when I had a possible choice of 150 other seats on the aeroplane.

- Receiving a cheque for money which I was owed, 18 months after the event and yet only 12 hours after I had, by chance, found a photo of the person involved. The amount I received was triple the original loan and arrived at a time when personal funds were low and therefore was much appreciated!

- Bumping into someone whom I hadn't seen for months but whom I had been talking about 10 minutes earlier. We met in the bustling streets of London after I had changed direction literally a few minutes before.

I am sure everybody can quote examples like these and they reinforce the Universal Law which states that when you are in tune with the core of your soul essence and living in the moment, the Universe **will always** supply the means and opportunities to fulfil your potential.

Our part of the bargain is to keep our eyes, ears and heart open and commit to following the intuitive urgings through to their natural conclusion.

Some would say that it is not that we attract these people or situations consciously but that we only see or hear what holds our interest at that time. So, when we buy a red car, we see only red cars on the road and when we decide to travel to Australia every newspaper we open has an article on the country. This is certainly true, but I would say that the essence of manifestation is the ability to direct our attention to those things which help us along our path which includes reflecting our truth in the world around us.

One of my favourite intuitive exercises is to invite Workshop participants to wander around the streets surrounding the venue with the instruction that there is a message waiting for them from their intuition which they will see or hear within 20 minutes.

I ask them to keep their minds and hearts open and to focus on a particular question which is uppermost in their thoughts at this time. I remember clearly Debbie's experience. She was eager to leave her present job but unsure of her future. Due to financial insecurity she didn't want to be out of work for too long but she was also exhausted and needed a break.

She arrived back after the allocated time looking perplexed. 'I don't know', she said, 'As I walked I came face to face with a shoe shop where they repaired shoes. In the window was a large notice which said "Soles and heels while you wait". What does it mean?'

The group burst into laughter and one member said: 'Did you hear what you said? Souls heal while you wait!' She received her answer.

An interesting twist to the subject of synchronicity was first noticed several years ago when practitioners of *remote viewing* were researching ESP. Simple symbols randomly selected by a computer were sent telepathically to volunteers many miles away. The results were encouraging with over 70% of the recipients accurately drawing the chosen symbol.

However, what was extraordinary to the human mind was that many of the recipients detected their symbol three days *before* it was randomly selected by the computer. This anomaly defies our understanding of communication being a consecutive event and forces us to expand our consciousness beyond that which is considered logical.

Finally:

It has been said that if we feel excited by something, it has already happened on some plane of existence and our sense of anticipation is purely our soul resonating with that truth and opening the way for the idea to become reality.

This suggests that if we feel **no** excitement for an event, or indeed there is anxiety, then we need to change our attitude or change what we are doing, for when excitement and joy are expressed there is a deepening of the connection to the eternal flame of our being.

This brings us nicely to a few forms of manifestation which are popular amongst those in the know!

Parking Spaces and Green Lights　Here the will is used to manifest parking spaces or to change the traffic lights to green with, in the majority of cases, a high level of emotional energy involved:

'Please let there be a parking space . . . please!'

When we are successful we are delighted; when the space fails to materialise we usually find convincing reasons why the space was not available **this** time.

'The walk is good for me'.
'I was probably being saved from a meteorite which was about to crash into that space'.
'My mind was wandering. I wasn't concentrating!'

Cloud Zapping　During part of my spiritual journey in the USA I could be found lying on my back concentrating on wisps of cloud which slowly glided across the almost perfect blue sky. I was *cloud zapping* believing that I could *will* any cloud to disperse; I had some positive results although a cynic would say that the moisture just evaporated.

Somehow on my return to England I failed to engender the same enthusiasm for cloud zapping when staring up at a completely grey sky!

These exercises are an essential part of the intuitive journey which help us to appreciate the power of the mind and the belief that through focused direction we can create our own reality. However, once we've learnt these lessons, it's time to move on, knowing that when we are flowing with our soul intention, parking spaces, green lights and many others things *naturally* fall into place *at the right time* and we will be in no doubt that the time is right!

If we continue to manipulate energy purely for pleasure or for petty personal needs then the sense of power which is experienced can go to our head and we start to believe that we can manipulate the Universe to supply all our needs whenever we choose. Our motivation then becomes twisted and we are one step closer to transforming *White Magic* into *Black Magic*. This may sound melodramatic but power corrupts and although today it may only be the manipulation of traffic lights, tomorrow it may be the world!

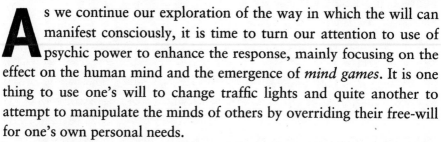

7 Harnessing the will: continued

Easy is the way down to the Underworld:
by night and by day Hades' door stands open;
but to retrace one's steps and to make a way out to the
upper air,
that's the task, that is the labour

Virgil, *Aeneid*, 70–19 BC

The will and psychic power

As we continue our exploration of the way in which the will can manifest consciously, it is time to turn our attention to use of psychic power to enhance the response, mainly focusing on the effect on the human mind and the emergence of *mind games*. It is one thing to use one's will to change traffic lights and quite another to attempt to manipulate the minds of others by overriding their free-will for one's own personal needs.

It concerns me when someone openly admits that they can *'make other people do as they please'*. The concern is less for myself and more for their depth of delusion and its effect on those who are more gullible.

Such mind control is the basis of *voodoo* and curses but is not restricted to primitive tribes. It is present in every society especially where there is intense competition and a perceived threat to survival. It may be subtle as in clever advertising, glossy brochures, tempting offers and subliminal messages or be more direct, accompanied by threats.

When the battle of wills is fought using the tools of logic and persuasion then refusal to concede usually puts a stop to the offensive. However, when the will is allied to the psychic powers which defy logic, social graces and morality are often abandoned.

The psychic field is an accumulation of all the thoughts and emotions which have ever been expressed and is a rich source of energy which can be employed creatively, or destructively, depending on the intention of the user. Many view this arena with a suspicion bordering on fear because of its failure to follow a logical pattern and because it is seen, incorrectly, as a place that only the selective few can enter. The truth is that we all enter this world in our dreams, including day dreams but in the majority of cases it is not a conscious decision.

By using the channels of the astral, psychic or fourth dimension which defy time and space, it is possible for an individual to project thoughts, sounds, lights, objects and even an image of themselves wherever they choose. This is a natural tool and something which has been used by the Ancient Peoples to increase their connection with each other and with their Source.

However, those who indulge in mind games with the aid of psychic tools purely to increase their own personal power know exactly what they are doing and are playing with fire, abusing the power which was given to them by the Creator.

Fortunately, the gift of free-will prevents anyone from being able to override the will of another **unless** there has been an agreement between the two individuals which, in most cases, is implied rather than formal. It is too late to cry *foul* when the end-result is not what we expected; if we choose to step into the psychic arena then we need to be fully aware of the *ghosts and demons* which we may encounter, many of which reflect our own shadow.

From the observer's perspective, it is also important to be aware of our own motives when judging others who we consider are playing mind games for our sense of disapproval and outrage can inadvertently add *fuel* to the contest.

Psychic attack

In this situation the individual describes a feeling of being mentally, energetically and occasionally physically attacked during their sleeping or waking moments without there being any actual physical violation on the part of their assailant.

Before discussing what action can be taken when under such attack, it is important to understand the value of this phase of the journey for our spiritual evolution, otherwise at this point there will be a strong temptation to turn round and run back to base.

As we regain our power and feel the core of our being strengthen from within, we will meet various challenges associated with the use of this power and will be asked to make conscious decisions rather than blame our unconscious for most of our actions.

These challenges include:

- Meeting those who attempt to *rob us of our free-will* through threats and criticism. Hopefully, rather than accepting defeat, we will meet the challenge with defiance and resolve to stand our ground and refuse to yield.
- Encountering those who subtly *offer our ego tempting rewards* if we agree to combine forces and drain us of our power to further their own needs.
- Attracting towards us situations which are personally destructive and appear *evil* so as *to recognise that part of ourselves* which is lost within the shadows.

Here are examples of each of these situations with solutions which may help you in the future:

1 Strengthening of free-will   I had always believed that as a doctor I was honour bound to act and appear in a certain way as befitted this role in society. But one day I was taught that this rather self-inflated image of myself could only lead to disaster as it led to expectations out of my reach and separated me from my true self.

My *teacher* came in the disguise of a colleague who, without provocation, attacked me saying that he had always believed that I was kind, caring and spiritual but that now all he could see was my darkness. I was shocked especially as we had been friends and I began to question my inner state and whether I had been deluding myself all the time.

At the same time I felt my energy begin to drain away until something inside told me that this attack was psychic in origin and that his *arrow* had found a tear in my aura which had been created by my own ego. Without a further thought I said: 'If that is how you see me that is fine but I will not own the darkness'. Immediately the loss of energy ceased and he knew that I hadn't fallen for his trick; he became very submissive and said: 'You're right, I've had a bad day today'.

But our relationship never returned to its previous state and I am today still grateful to him for helping me to shed the facade of conditioning which I had worn for so long.

2 The temptations of the ego   Many years ago I was invited to join an elite group run by two women who explained that they were performing important work for the planet. I was immediately hooked as the offer provided all the allure I desired.

But, as the weeks went by, I realised that I was being asked to do more and more and saw little evidence of their contribution. Then, after one particularly tiring session, I had a psychic dream where I saw myself behind a glass screen watching these women stab a defenceless individual.

Waking in a sweat and with my pulse racing, I knew their victim was me and that I was witnessing our relationship on a more sinister level. That day I returned their books and learnt that the desires of the ego must not overrule the pure intentions of the soul.

3 Meeting our shadow   A few years later, I had a period of unexplained phenomena affecting my home, mind and body which caused me great anxiety. If I had described my symptoms to a fellow doctor, they would have probably sent me to see a psychiatrist and yet somewhere inside I knew I was sane and that this was an initiatory stage of my journey.

I sought the help of a highly qualified psychotherapist who was recommended as having a spiritual outlook but, unfortunately, she had no idea what I was talking about and tried to convince me that my anxiety was due to a heavy work schedule.

Following that encounter, I decided to keep my own counsel and asked for help and protection from my higher self and soul family. I wrapped myself in white light, lit candles, burnt powerful cleansing incense, sent love to the source of the attack and invoked guidance through prayer.

One morning in meditation I received a message to look within myself for that part of me which created the fear. Almost immediately my inner vision showed me a sad, wizened woman who used black magic to gain control, increase her power and demand respect. When I spoke to this sub-personality, I realised that such a life style develops from feelings of rejection, inadequacy and lack of love.

Despite the enormous hold she had on my psyche, her request was simple; she wanted to be loved. This simple gift transformed this essential power from a chaotic force to one which I could use for the Greater Good. Within hours of this powerful meditation, I felt a huge cloud had passed over, my soul was lighter and the phenomena stopped.

We all need to step into the psychic world in order to see and appreciate its strengths and weaknesses, taking from it the skills and expertise which will ease our spiritual journey as well as enhance the opportunities offered.

I perceive that psychospiritual disharmony will become more common in the future and that it is important that those who train to become experts in this field, understand that many disturbances of the mind are psychic and not purely related to this particular life or plane of existence. Indeed, modern surveys show that 10% of the population have experienced a Near Death Experience, whilst 40% believe they have seen a ghost.

The time has come to discuss these matters openly and to interface with the spirit world rather than just seeing them as distant relatives with whom we have nothing in common. I know many people whose childhood experiences of *playing with little friends, talking to their grandmother at the foot of their bed* and *seeing auras* were dismissed as fanciful, leading to the loss of a powerful sensory tool which can be as great a handicap as losing the power of sight or hearing.

To compensate, the logical left brain predominates, over-analysing everything and leaving nothing to chance. But the present change in global consciousness is reactivating this childhood knowledge which, with gentle coaxing, can only bring greater joy and fulfilment into our life.

The will and love

This is the purest form of manifestation where the intention is the will which has risen above the needs of the individual and acts as a laser to focus the Universal Will. Here there is no judgement or attachment to the result and on its own can appear rather cold and calculating but, when it is allied to the power of love, the result is amazing.

With an open heart, the individual enters a partnership with the object of manifestation. No force is required but instead there is a merging of energy fields as the manifestor takes on the essence of the object of creation. Hence, if a wise man wants to make it rain, he must first change the frequency of his being to that of water and humbly request that the rain should fall. In a similar way *telekinesis*, or the ability to move objects, takes place through a 'union' between the object and the operator.

This is true intuition where the mind enters the multi-dimensional levels and yet still holds a clearly defined focus of intention and where the heart is open and in total harmony with the heart-beat of the Universe. In this state there is an undeniable *knowing*.

Prior to this, we meet those who are still functioning from a place of *believing* which involves a closed heart and the need to use the strength of will to bring about manifestation by shattering and rearranging the energy bonds which can lead to unpredictable results.

Love is the answer and is more powerful than any mental energy.

By merging their will with the will of the Divine, a number of gifted individuals are able to materialise healing oils, metals, ash, voices, flowers and other significant objects in order to enhance their teaching or healing powers. These experts in materialisation have usually been chosen specifically from amongst their own people and have been expected to undergo rigorous personal trials and deprivations so as to purify their intention.

Hence we observe the shamans and medicine men and women who, by altering the frequency of their energy field, can manifest symbolically forms which have a significant meaning in their tradition. Therefore, in the case of disease, the patient may actually see insects, snakes, fluids, demonic forms and dark shapes leaving their body, offering them the evidence they require to believe that they are cured of their illness.

Psychic surgeons work in a very similar way altering their energy field to allow them to enter through the physical body of their patient and to perform *operations* within the subtle realms. They are seen to remove seemingly *diseased tissue* whilst leaving little external evidence of their intervention. It is possible that they produce this tissue purely for effect in keeping with the idea that many people still need visual proof of spiritual matters.

All these individuals work from a loving heart and their highest wisdom, laying aside the needs of their ego. However, there are charlatans in every field and I am reminded of a story told to me by a friend who encountered a man professing to be a spiritual teacher but who appeared to have become blinded by the glamour such abilities can bring:

> 'Look, I can produce oil in my hand' he said proudly.
> 'What good is that to the Universe?' my friend asked; he had no answer.
> He tried again: 'Look I can produce gold in my hand'.
> 'What good is that to the Universe?' she retorted.
> He went away feeling deflated that his tricks had failed to impress.
> Later that night he appeared in her room using astral travel.
> 'Look I can travel anywhere I choose' he said, playing his trump card.
> 'What good is that to the Universe?' she calmly replied.

The only difference between a trick and a miracle is the intent of the performer. The ability to manifest is a wonderful gift which is God given and should not be abused. The greater the gift the greater the risk of becoming blinded by the lustre of glamour and power. These talents can be taught but it is inherent in any spiritual teacher to teach first the values of humility, respect and accountability and be a true example of their instruction.

Finally, there are manifestations or dematerialisations which emerge from a collaboration between our intuition and our spirit guides, and are used to emphasise a particular message. These episodes will appear throughout our journey although in the early stages we may fail to see the signs or be unable to decipher the code. Through practice comes skill and the more we understand the nature of our intuition the easier it is to read the messages. Let me give you some of my examples:

Signs of enlightenment

A few years ago I was driving to a conference where I was to give a talk on 'Letting your Inner Light Shine'. As I pulled into a Service Area I was pleased to rest from the thick fog which had hampered my vision on the Motorway. Walking away from the car, another driver shouted: 'Your lights are still on'.

'They can't be', I replied 'I've just switched them off'. Returning to the car, I was dismayed to find that even though the off-switch had been activated, the lights still shone brightly and I realised that unless I sought help, the car's battery would eventually become flat. Fortunately, I found a garage mechanic who replaced the errant switch allowing me to regain control over the function of the lights.

The audience, later in the day, found my tale very amusing especially when I told them that the accompanying communication from my higher self said: 'If you don't rest and switch off your lights once in a while, your inner battery will become exhausted'. The message struck home and I learnt to trust that my guides will use every opportunity to get their message across!

Dematerialisation

I am now convinced there is a large *black hole* somewhere containing an assortment of objects which have mysteriously disappeared from my life without trace even though I would swear on oath that I had left them in a safe place.

There is the airline ticket which disappeared finally convincing me to cancel a journey which I had been determined to take even though others had advised me against it. There are pieces of jewellery with specific personal value which went missing overnight, having been carefully placed on the cabinet at the side of the bed.

Later one piece reappeared on a similar cabinet but now in a hotel room. This suggested some interference by the spirit world and provided evidence of materialisation defying time and space.

Then there was my manuscript on *Clinical Medicine* which was to be basis of a book for complementary practitioners. One minute it was lying on my desk and the next it had disappeared. Despite an intensive search it was never found and my higher guidance told me 'This is not the book we want you to write. There is a far more important one to be written'. And out of that came my first book *Frontiers of Health*.

Spirit friends who come as messengers and healers

This story was told to me by a friend. Many years ago she had suddenly developed a serious illness with stiffness of the joints, high temperatures and extreme lethargy. Her condition baffled the doctors who, after running many tests, could not reach a diagnosis and could only prescribe symptomatic relief which failed to accelerate her speed of recovery. One night, at about 3 o'clock, as she lay in her hospital bed feeling wretched with the rigors and the sweats, she saw through the ward's dimmed lights, a young doctor standing at the bottom of her bed.

She hadn't noticed him before amongst the staff and imagined he was a locum for the night who had been called to the ward for another patient. His eyes were clear and bright and she seemed to lose herself in the brightness of his smile. He gently reached for her hand and, after asking a few questions relevant to the illness, reassured her that she would soon be well and left.

When the nurses came to wash her in the morning they were amazed to find her sitting up in bed with a normal temperature. 'My goodness, that was a quick recovery', they exclaimed.

'I don't know what happened, but I felt so much better after I spoke to the young doctor', she explained.

The nurses looked at each other in puzzlement: 'What young doctor? We haven't seen anybody else all night'.

It then dawned on my friend that her visitor had been no ordinary medical specialist but possessed qualifications exclusive to the Spiritual Realms.

Discarnate entities

The last story takes us nicely onto the subject of discarnate entities. Throughout our journey, the majority of the spirit world is helping, supporting and guiding us. However, there are factions of this dimension whose intentions are less objective, mainly due to the fact that they exist very close to this planet's vibration and therefore are still driven by many of the habits and desires which they displayed whilst on Earth.

They tend to be attracted to individuals with similar inclinations or where there is a strong emotional attachment and can lead to changes in behaviour and thought interference. In most cases they wish no harm although those on the Earth plane may view the experience in a very different light.

This type of *possession* is rare with the majority of 'mind control' resulting from negative beliefs we hold about ourselves which emerge from deep within our own subconscious. However, to prevent any type of possession we need to:

- Wake up and take control
- Love, honour and respect ourself and then the ways of others
- Walk the path of our own Truth
- Let our Inner Light shine
- Believe in ourself with a healthy self-esteem

Possession occurs when *the lights are on and nobody is at home*! Remaining asleep throughout life, playing power games, developing through limiting beliefs and using one's will detrimentally, all increase the possibility of possession, which may be expressed in the following ways:

1 Thoughtforms   As discussed previously, we tend to create thought-forms in relation to our own experiences, social teaching and global knowledge. The strongest form is that which relates to our belief about ourselves which tends to act as a template for future manifestation.

These personal beliefs can also attract towards us thoughtforms which circulate in the lower mental dimensions of the collective consciousness causing us to feel as if we are enveloped in an extremely sticky substance where there is no freedom to move. Indeed, we may identify these thoughts as emanating from a particular individual who has died and consequently believe that they are in some way controlling us.

However, in most cases, the thoughtform belongs to us and during the life of that individual they simply reinforced our own belief. Therefore, by transforming our self-image to something more positive and loving, the so-called possession usually stops.

2 Ethereal Communication   Sometimes a loved one from the other side wants to make their presence known and offer support and guidance. This can be extremely comforting, especially when the individuals concerned shared a common belief in an after-life. However, sometimes, in their eagerness to communicate or help, the contact occurs suddenly causing fear or may fail to respect the feelings of the recipient.

In most cases, the non-physical being can easily be persuaded to *'withdraw'* and allow space or to find a more suitable way of making contact such as during the dream state. However, expert help may be required if these simple requests are not met.

3 Earthbound Beings   When we die, we initially pass to the level of awareness which complements the world of consciousness we have just left. Therefore, if we are obsessed with the material world we will be guided to a similar environment, close to the Earth plane until we are ready to accept the larger picture.

This may mean that we remain in a particular location without a physical body, as in the case of *ghosts*, waiting to be released from our earthbound existence. Poltergeists are a type of ghost, attracted towards those whose energies are unstable or immature, such as teenagers. They use the energy of the individual to power their tricks, often causing objects to move mysteriously.

For some beings, their addiction to food, smoking, drugs and alcohol will naturally keep them bound to places on this Earth where their habits can be satisfied. They cluster around pubs, drug haunts, raves and other meetings waiting for someone to become unconscious or become ungrounded so that they can move in. Without a physical form, they cannot taste the essence of their addiction but can, through the unconscious addict, experience the emotional and psychological changes which take place during a *high*.

When the individual awakens, they depart.

Similar possession occasionally arises in chronic mental illness although it is more common to find these individuals surrounded by their own negative thoughtforms. It is easy to see that there is a tremendous need to appreciate the complexity of mental illness taking research beyond genetic inheritance, chemical imbalance and social up-bringing.

4 Other Absent Owners   Partial possession can also occur when an individual is unconscious, even for a short time, such as following a head injury or during a general anaesthetic. After the event, friends and family may notice a change in behaviour or moods which, despite medical examination, fails to reveal any pathological cause

Although incidents of possession post-general anaesthetic are extremely rare, it is wise to draw the *white light* around you before you go 'off to sleep' as well as positively affirming that the operation will go well, you trust the surgeon and anaesthetist, your vital signs will remain stable, blood loss will be minimal, the need for pain relief will be low and you will recover quickly and fully.

I doubt if any negative energies could infiltrate this shield of love and faith!

5 Walk-ins   In order to complete this section, I want to mention *walk-ins*. These are discarnate beings who have apparently made a contract with a soul on earth that, at a certain age, the latter will vacate their body to this new entity. Through this ready-made life, it is believed that the new occupant can offer a particular service to humanity. Some suggest that the in-coming being is extra-terrestrial but my comment would be 'Who isn't?'.

The change-over naturally leads to a transformation in personality which is recognised by friends and family. From speaking to those who work with all types of possession, I understand that walk-in is very rare and most cases actually fall within one of the previous categories.

Rescue work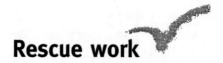

Most *lost souls* want to leave this earthly plane and return to their soul path. From our side, we can help by surrounding the discarnate being in white light and praying to those on the other side that they may come close and lead the soul into the Light.

In certain cases, expertise may be required from someone who works specifically with lost souls who are reluctant to leave. Such an expert may be found within a religious setting or be a sensitive or psychic who has dedicated their life to this service. Through their skills, which may include exorcism, the discarnate being eventually finds its way home.

Ritual and rhythm

So much of this chapter has been dedicated to the *right use of power*, attempting to show that it is only through close attention to our intuition that we can feel the deep reverberations of our being and, from this, can *sound* our own personal moral code which will become the motivation behind all our actions.

The more we vibrate with the rhythm of our soul, the more we attract those with whom we are in harmony. In other words when we find ourselves, we find our point of unity with all souls.

**Experience the joy of singing your own song and
you will hear the choir.**

One of the ways in which we can find this natural balance is through the development of rituals which help us to define the parameters of our existence without limiting our soul potential. Ritual realigns us to the rhythm of our being, the rhythm of the Earth and the rhythm of the Universe. Outside the *beat of this drum* there is chaos and the path of 'right living' is far less easy to define.

All religions employ ritual, recognising its essential role in reconnecting the soul to its Creator. Throughout our day we carry out rituals, starting with the habits which we employ on rising in the morning. Do you shower before making a drink or after you've let the dog out? Do you like to read the newspaper in the morning or save it for later in the day, preferring to meditate before the rest of the house wakens? We all need these routines in order to focus our attention on the day ahead and to provide a sense of continuity and security in our life.

However, ritual can develop into an obsession when it is seen as the goal rather than the means. I have often witnessed individuals becoming so involved with creating the *right* atmosphere that they lose their way and allow fear to drive them rather than love. When things don't work out they add another ritual to their already busy schedule and eventually become exhausted. This addictive behaviour often hides a fear of moving forward and the need to release old, redundant beliefs.

Ritual is a tool which attracts, focuses and magnifies intent in a similar manner to a crystal which intensifies the information which passes through it in the field of electronics. It is not the ritual which is important but the **intent** behind its use. Throughout history we have seen rituals used to increase the power of individuals and groups, but it is only in retrospect that we can see whether their motivation was beneficial or destructive to humanity as a whole.

At this time in our evolution, ritual is becoming increasingly important to our way of life as reflected in the expanding interest in shamanistic teachings, the traditions of the Native Americans, the use of crystals, sound and colour and the development of sacred space. However:

It is not the rattle or the drum which brings us closer to our truth but our willingness to walk the path of the intuition and to find ourselves along the way.

Only then can the individual consciously choose to merge their will with the will of the many.

As we complete this stage of the journey, we recognise ourselves as stronger, wiser and better able to withstand the glamour which naturally accompanies self-awareness.

Exercises to work in harmony with the will

The following exercises are steps which help us to develop a healthy relationship with our will and set the scene for clarity of thought and a pure heart.

1 Relaxation of the body   This can be achieved through progressive muscle relaxation or by allowing the muscles to relax with each breath. Through practice this can become a natural condition rather than just a procedure practised at the ends of the day.

2 Entering a state of meditation   As discussed previously, meditation changes the frequency of the brain waves thereby allowing the individual to assess other levels of awareness. Mantras, music and concentrating on the breath or an image greatly enhance the ability to achieve this place of stillness.

Eventually, one hopes to achieve a dynamic state of meditation as is seen in the Buddhist practice of *Mindfulness* (see bibliography), where we can live in the present moment whilst being open to other dimensions.

3 Becoming aware of our surroundings.   From this place of stillness we can then allow our senses to scan our environment and pick up any nuances which may be relevant to our spiritual life at that moment. This is performed without judgement or emotional attachment and it is useful to keep a journal and make notes of your observations.

Become aware of episodes of synchronicity in your life and see whether there is a particular state of mind which tends to attract these events.

i.e. *Were you meditating, praying, relaxing or was it just a passing thought?*

4 Opening your heart to the world around you   This is easier to achieve in meditation than in everyday life especially when we are stressed. Next time you feel tense, take a deep breath and release it, lower your shoulders and move your awareness to the area of your heart and allow the love within to dissolve the tension. Now when you speak or act, let it be from the place of the compassionate observer.

5 Allowing your environment to 'speak' to you   *Think of a question which is uppermost in your thoughts at this time. Prepare yourself by becoming relaxed and centred and ask your question.*

Taking a pen and paper with you, go outside if you are indoors. Walk until something on your path attracts your attention. You may even pass the *answer* but an inner awareness will draw you back to the same spot. Focus on the object which has caught your eye. Make a note of your findings.

Ask your inner wisdom for a clear interpretation of the message in relation to your present situation and make further notes. (The exercise should take less than 20 minutes).

When you are ready, give thanks, return to your starting point and allow the information you received to assist you along your path enhanced by a heightened sense of inner strength and certainty.

8 Taking a stand: making decisions from one's inner truth

The man who is denied the opportunity of taking decisions of importance begins to regard as important the decisions he is allowed to take.

C. Northcote Parkinson, *Parkinson's Law,* **1958**

With our travel bags almost overflowing with knowledge, the final stages of our journey rely upon the insights we have gleaned along the way and challenge us to put our theories to the test and become a dynamic representation of our truth. The path itself transforms from a gently meandering trail to one which ascends steeply, requiring the pilgrim to apply all the skills they have acquired in order to secure a firm footing. Whereas on the more level sections, it was easy to allow the mind to wander from the actual process of walking, we now need to focus on each step employing our own inner guidance.

Although our progress may be slow and potentially stressful, the gift of being totally present in the moment creates an overwhelming sense of contentment and inner strength. As we climb higher and higher, we are granted the opportunity of viewing with reverence the rich landscape which radiates before us, seeing and experiencing far beyond our five senses.

During the climb we are presented with various obstacles which relate to earlier stages of the journey and which allow us to assess whether we have truly moved beyond that particular level of consciousness. The only problem is that like the game of *snakes and ladders*, as we approach the completion of our pilgrimage, there are fewer safe spaces between the snakes and due to the length of their bodies, we can slide back quite a distance before being allowed to stand up and walk forward again.

So as we place one foot in front of the other, it is important to be clear about our decision-making process in order to avoid the wily serpents which are lurking between the rocky crevices, remembering that any decision asks us to make a statement in relation to *something we believe at that time* which is based on a number of different factors.

As discussed previously, our beliefs or thoughtforms emerge from three different sources: those which are acquired, those which bring reason to an emotional experience and those, initiated by the intuition, which align us with our spiritual purpose. At this stage of the journey our decisions need to be created primarily from our intuition honouring all other options but with sufficient expertise to avoid becoming encumbered or deluded by any of them.

Decisions inspired by the intuition

The finest example of this is characterised by the wise man or woman of the tribe whether they represent an indigenous race or a large corporation. Their status brings with it a high level of authority and, at the same time, immense responsibility, which requires them to operate from an objective point of view rather than from one which satisfies their own personal need for gain. Surrounded by their people they listen intently, without interruption, to those who wish to air their views. Their senses are highly attuned to all levels of communication and hence, behind the spoken words, they hear the passionate appeals, the ego-based motives, the seductive requests, the angry cries and those who speak quietly and yet express a deeply held conviction.

Although they may have already formed their own opinion concerning the matter in hand, they place that to one side and listen with an open heart and mind, without judgement, and appreciate that all views contain a truth at some level. This is true detached compassion where there is **a willingness to assimilate all the information and then make a decision which will benefit the Spirit of the tribe as well as the individuals who contribute to that energy.**

It may be the case that after hearing all the views it is the leader's original sentiment which is implemented but this is a carefully selected choice and not one which indicates a dictatorial attitude.

Whenever we are in the presence of such a leader, who hears and acknowledges us as an individual with something to offer, we are more inclined to change our view to that which is for the common good than when we are disregarded, for then we tend to believe that any choice other than our own is the wrong one.

> *The Master is available to all people*
> *and doesn't reject anyone.*
> *He is ready to use all situations*
> *and doesn't waste anything.*
> *This is called embodying the Light*
>
> **Lao-tzu,** *Tao Te Ching,* **500 BC**

Inevitably, no solution will meet everybody's needs and there will always be those who disagree or feel unfairly treated. There are also those individuals who are fearful of taking any responsibility, especially for their own life, who take pleasure in sitting on *the sidelines.* They watch the proceedings, offer little to the general debate, fail to air their disagreement openly but will be the first to say: '*I told you so!*' when events take a downward turn.

Here, the wise person will listen but decline to be drawn into a power game preferring to keep their vision clear and their eye focused on the wider picture.

There are many who believe that they act already from an unemotional stance although it is easy to confuse this with an autocratic position where consultation and group discussion are discouraged. I suggest that this autonomous approach often conceals a fear of losing control which, due to its irrational, subconscious origin, makes any decision which arises, precarious. Before we can reach any solution through the intuitive channels, we first have to face our own demons within the shadows and learn to transform the power of negative emotions into a tremendous source of creative wealth.

An experience from my own life which exemplifies this matter of making decisions without consultation comes from my recent trip to Peru and involves a situation from many lives past. I was fortunate to be part of a large spiritual group which was introduced to the sacred sites through the eyes of an Inca messenger.

It was late and the sun had completely disappeared as we stood around the Medicine Wheel which is part of the Sacsayhuaman complex, just outside Cusco. Already the temperature was dropping and there was some urgency to descend to the plateau and find our coach which would return us to the hotel in the town. Equipped with only a few flashlights, we made our way down the complex system of steps and passageways.

As we reached ground level, I saw the lights of a coach in the car park in the distance and, believing this to be our transport, found myself leading the group in that direction. Unfortunately, when we arrived we found that the coach belonged to another tour and there was no sign of our vehicle. There was a general feeling of discouragement and confusion and without thinking, or consulting others, I left the group and headed off in the direction of the other car park about a quarter of a mile away. Just as I arrived, I saw our driver realising his mistake setting off to find his tourists.

Suffice to say, we did eventually all arrive back at the hotel for a welcome shower and hot meal. But I was fascinated by the whole event for, despite the dark night sky and the absence of any light, at no time did my feet falter as I ran across the stones, moats and rubble which covered the area.

That night I had a dream and saw myself as the leader of a large tribe. I was shown that, because of my ego, I had been too proud to consult with others at a crucial time in our history, leading to the death and suffering of many of my followers.

I believe that the dream related to the transition period between the civilisations of Lemuria and Atlantis which allowed me to realise that my overwhelming sense of duty in this life was a karmic throw back to this experience. The following day we entered a sacred cave where pilgrims come to ask for forgiveness. I took full advantage of the situation and, having made my request for clemency, enquired why I had carried this burden for so long. The reply which I received had a very simple message: *'Forgiveness was always available to you; you were just too proud to ask'*.

This lesson showed me that there were two main features in making a decision from the intuition:

1 Letting go of one's pride, opinions and judgement and, with an open heart and mind, listening to the views of all those concerned.

2 Assimilating all the information available and then from the overview of the intuition reach a decision by which you will stand.

So are you ready to *make decisions without fear or regret* from this place of wisdom and compassion? On the deepest level it often requires us to stand alone, to express an apparently illogical view or appear uncompromising, and yet there is nothing superficial about our decision as we reach across the divide and work in harmony with the Universal vision for the future.

The day of decision is the day to act upon it
Japanese Proverb

Let us consider the other options which are available in order to clarify our own process.

Decisions based on acquired knowledge

As we are now aware, knowledge which is learned has an important role to play in creating the structure and fabric of our society especially in relationship to our laws, statutes and moral codes. However, if all our decisions over the centuries had been based purely on what was already known, there would have been **no** advance in terms of technology, culture or consciousness.

Most inventions develop from *an inspired idea* outside the realms of reason although sometimes they can be the result of *a mistake* which is later recognised as a potential winner. The individuals involved are pioneers willing to step out from the crowd and commonly become a source of ridicule to their scientific friends. They employ more than logic; there is often a passion for discovery, a love for the unexpected and the wisdom to know when they are in the presence of a *priceless gem* or when they hold a *piece of fool's gold*.

> **Their talents embrace the intuitive qualities without which mankind has no future.**

Decisions related to the emotions

Many of our decisions are still influenced by our emotions, especially fear, even though there may be a facade of logic. The *snakes* we meet at this level usually reflect these emotions, and are strongly connected to old patterns of behaviour, which prevent us from standing in our truth by weakening the force of our soul intention.

So, instead of making choices based on reasoning and insight, we make decisions strongly connected to an ulterior motive or heavily loaded with subtle emotional blackmail:

> *'If I decide to do this, maybe he/she'll like/approve/support/stay with me'.*

At other times, decisions can be driven by fear such as the fear of failure which can paralyse us from making any resolve:

> *'What if it doesn't work?'*
> *'What if I'm wrong?'*

We can also enlist the help and support of our intellect to create one **excuse** after another so as to prevent us from ever having to make a definitive statement in our life:

'I'd love to but . . . '.
'I just can't find anything which suits me'.
'If I was more intelligent/richer/less busy, then I would love to join you'.
'When my children leave home/I'm better qualified/have more money, then I'll . . . '.

Ultimately, we can find ourselves becoming driven by superstition, creating an illogical logic with a huge emotional bias, believing that if we act in a certain way others will be negatively affected or that the disapproval of others can influence the result of our decisions:

*'I don't want to have him in my team and yet I'm afraid that his exclusion could **jinx** our success'.*

So we end up seeking the support and approval of others for our decisions partly for encouragement and partly to spread the blame when things go wrong!

Even when we do make a decision and follow through on it, we can still allow our emotions to obscure the result, forfeiting valuable nurturing and growth for the soul.

'I feel so guilty; I wish I hadn't started this.'
'I didn't know that things would change so much.'
'I feel so guilty that I am so happy!'

Many of these statements involve power games although they are now occurring on a more conscious level and with a greater degree of wilfulness. Interestingly, the contestants have also changed with less external participation and with the main contest taking place between our lower self and our soul essence or in other words between *My will versus Thy will.*

The emotions are a powerful source of energy which at this stage of the climb should be working with us and not dragging us down into the abyss of despair. Through meditation it is important to reassure the lower self or personality that its anxieties have been heard and that the strengthening trust in the intuition is successfully leading us towards a less chaotic state of mind and greater peace.

Finally, it helps to re-frame our thoughts, which loosens the emotional bonds and allows us to stand tall and confident in our own sense of conviction. Hence we may:

- Transform fear into excitement
- Turn *a lack of support* from others into *the freedom to be oneself*
- Use disapproval either as the leverage to act or the ability to accept the views of others and still walk one's path
- Encourage those we love to follow their own intuition
- Celebrate when we follow through on a decision, before any assessment of the result

The responsibility that comes with making decisions

With every decision there is a responsibility which increases proportionately in relation to the level of perceived or actual authority. This is a theme I know well from my chosen career, which I might say offers enormous spiritual rewards but at a high cost to the emotional and physical health of the doctor. There are few professions where one's decision can mean life or death to someone in one's care and where responsibility is almost completely handed over to the expert from the very start of the relationship.

Nevertheless, when I passed through the doors of the Medical School, I was willing to take on that mantle of responsibility although, in retrospect, as an eighteen year old I had little understanding of what this meant in reality. Through the years I was asked to make decisions based on the knowledge I had accumulated from books, lectures, the senior medical profession, my own experiences and from the wisdom of patients. But, in the heat of the moment and at the dead of night, it was my intuition which guided me through the most difficult and complex situations towards a solution which I was prepared to stand by – whatever the consequences.

I can remember sitting at the bedside of a woman in labour whilst around me the world slept. The only other person awake was the baby, suspended within the womb, which minute by minute was becoming an extremely hazardous place to remain. I knew that I had to make the decision very shortly as to whether this mother could deliver the baby naturally or whether I should set the wheels in motion and prepare for a Caesarean Section.

Perhaps those who work in *high-tech* medicine would laugh at my dilemma, wondering why this woman had not been taken to the operating theatre during a scheduled session in the daytime. However, I still believe that birth is not a disease but a natural process and, with professional care and attention, we can create a setting where we achieve optimal results for all concerned.

In the end, I made my decision based on my experience and on a strong inner conviction that this baby would be born naturally which indeed was the case. But I knew that we three (the mother, the baby and I) had shared the responsibility for the birth, each contributing our own expertise and our innate understanding of health and this I believe is the way forward for health care.

At this present time, in almost every so-called developed country, we find a *knee jerk reaction* to any fault, mistake, mishap or disaster which occurs, with everybody looking for somebody else to blame. The level of litigation is increasing rapidly leading to:

- Soaring insurance premiums
- Tough legislation across the board which attempts to eliminate any margin of error
- Heightened fear of stepping outside one's defined parameters
- A decrease in the service offered especially at the point of contact so as to limit the period of time when liability is a risk

This is an unhealthy state of affairs which stifles creativity, spiritual growth, heart connection and community spirit and can only be resolved when each individual is willing to take responsibility for their own decisions which includes asking for help from an expert. I see a future where instead of procuring defensive insurance, a contract is drawn up where every party is committed to give of their best at that time, using all their skills and expertise and finally sealing the agreement with love and respect.

I hope, for the sake of all of us, that this day is not far away.

A final story was told to me by Denise who attended a seminar. It is a fine example of someone who weighed up all the options, made her decision and was then prepared to stand by her truth, despite the consequences.

Denise had known her friend since schooldays and when they both got married the friendship continued and widened to embrace the families involved, with Denise becoming godmother to her friend's eldest son. As the years passed she was saddened to see the boy become involved with a group of 'unsuitable' friends and yet pleased that he still came to visit her.

On one occasion, after he left she noticed that there was £40 missing from her purse but thought that she must have miscalculated her housekeeping money. However, when more money disappeared after subsequent visits she became suspicious and, on reflection, remembered that on a number of occasions, the boy had appeared twitchy and restless but had put it down to normal teenage energy.

With great regret, she came to the conclusion that it was probably her godson who had taken the money and that drugs may be involved. She thought long and hard about what to do. One part of her wanted to pretend that it had never happened, but that was not an option. She wondered if she could confront the boy without his parents knowing but he was still young and she didn't know if he would just deny the whole affair and carry on.

She eventually decided to talk to her friend and lay the whole scene before her. Initially, the mother defended her son and was outraged by the 'accusation' of theft but slowly other pieces of the jigsaw fell into place and the inevitable realisation that the boy was on drugs could no longer be avoided.

Unfortunately, the ordeal over the ensuing months took its toll on the women's friendship as the family closed ranks and it never really rallied. The godson entered a recovery programme and the friend went for counselling.

However, despite the outcome, when we met, Denise had no regret as to her decision for she still believes that she laid aside her ego and acted for the greater good from a place of unconditional love and would make the same decision again.

If we choose to embrace the power of Spirit which is being offered to all of us at this time, and receive its benefits, we need also to be willing to accept responsibility for our thoughts, words and deeds, including our mistakes. But we will find that the inner strength and sense of purpose which emerges from agreeing to such a challenge is beyond anything which we have experienced in the past.

Exercise to clarify our decisions

Choose a subject on which you are seeking to make a decision in your life.

Take three pieces of paper and write on one: *EMOTION*, the next: *LOGIC* and the last, *INTUITION*.

Depending on the space available, place them in three different locations around the room or even in three separate rooms.

Now, with pen and paper at hand, stand or sit close by the piece of paper marked *EMOTION* and connect with your emotional guidance and ask:

'What advice would you give me in order for me to make the best decision for all concerned?'

Write down your answer spending no longer than five minutes at the site.

Move to the place of *LOGIC* and then *INTUITION* tuning into the appropriate guidance and asking the relevant question.

Having received all the information assimilate the advice.

Ultimately, it is the guidance of our intuition we wish to follow but the emotions and logic can give useful advice and should be heeded unless they appear contradictory to the inner wisdom. By changing the location in which we receive the messages, we are inviting our consciousness to change also and to observe the situation from a different viewpoint thus providing the widest possible picture.

9 Letting go of the result: detached compassion

Therefore the Master takes action by letting things take their course
He remains as calm at the end as at the beginning
He has nothing, thus has nothing to lose.
What he desires is non-desire; what he learns is to unlearn
He simply reminds people of who they have always been

Lao-tzu, *Tao Te Ching,* **500 BC**

With the end of our journey in sight, the path is easier and we envision that at any moment all will become clear and we will know ourselves, our true purpose and our God. However, the anticipation we experience exposes one of the final tests of initiation for the pilgrim; the ability to let go of the expectations which surround the result of our activities. Only in this way can we become a living example of detached compassion where we reside in love without growing attached to that love or its outcome.

This is not the same as being *uncaring* or *disinterested* which are characteristically seen in those who fear commitment, vulnerability and rejection. This is a state of being totally present in any situation without distractions or expectations and yet, when the event is over, being able to move on without negative emotional attachment.

The importance to the Universe of this talent is that it can plant a seed of inspiration into our mind which, trusting our inner guidance, we will see through to its appropriate conclusion whilst also being sufficiently flexible to permit plans to change without experiencing great emotional turmoil or requiring lengthy discussion.

It is therefore not unusual at this stage of the journey to find ourselves being tested with respect to our degree of adaptability and our willingness to release all expectations, listening only to our intuition. One particular episode which reflects this challenge in my life occurred a few years ago when a series of events persuaded me to look for a Marketing Agent in order to reach across the Atlantic with my work. I *'put a message out'* to the Universe that I needed someone who knew the Mind/Body market in the USA and immediately met someone from Canada!

Even though my manifestation skills were marginally off-track, I eagerly agreed to tour the Toronto area during May of the following year. In the meantime, I was inwardly advised to study the Mayan culture which involved a trip to Central America, including Belize. Having completed my bookings for this pilgrimage, I set off for the teaching tour in Canada.

Although the first week went relatively well, the second was a disaster. Students failed to arrive at the appointed time, I was sent to the wrong address, we were locked out of the classroom and I can still remember standing in a telephone box relating my tale of woe to a friend, whilst feeling very sorry for myself. She was offering me a string of useful suggestions when out of the blue I received an inner message which said: *'You are not here to teach, there is something else you need to see'*, and I knew I was back on the trail!

Quickly, I thanked my friend and walked out into the warm Summer evening with a lighter step and the knowledge that all was well. The following day I was browsing in a book shop when a stranger approached me and said that she had to tell me about the crystal skull. Having been in the psychic/spiritual field for a long time, initially I was not impressed by her offer suspecting another trinket or modern healing tool. Then she added: *'It's Mayan'* at which point shivers ran up and down my spine.

My new friend told me about Anna Mitchell-Hedges, who is the keeper of the crystal skull which was found in Belize over 70 years ago. It is estimated to be at least 20,000 years old, made from pure quartz crystal and, anatomically, is an almost perfect replica of a human skull with a detachable lower jaw and all the sockets for the teeth. There are many stories concerning this and other crystal skulls and there is little doubt that they are sacred to our civilisation probably linking us to higher wisdom and a greater understanding of our origins and our role in the Universal Plan.

Anna's home was only 20 minutes from Toronto and as I sat before the crystal, transfixed by the beauty and eternal perfection of the skull, I started to appreciate my invitation to Canada. During my visit I was asked to take photographs of the skull to the people of the village where it had been found. I welcomed the thought of becoming a special envoy and happily changed my travel plans to include Lubaantun in the south of Belize.

From the beginning of the trip there were many episodes of synchronicity and therefore, when I eventually arrived in the village, I was brimming with excitement. Well, as the saying goes: 'Pride goes before a fall' and I was brought down to earth with a bang! Many of the elders who knew Anna in her early days were now dead and recent archaeological findings had eclipsed the events of the 1920s.

That night as I lay under the mosquito net in my Mayan dwelling, I pondered on the next step of this adventure. The following day I visited the ancient site and met the guides who were employed to take care of the temples and the surrounding land. Sitting with them under a tree sheltering from the midday sun, we shared stories and they told me of their medicine men and women, the healing gifts of certain plants and of the power of curses. In return, they asked me to explain *dowsing* and Earth energies as many experts on these subjects had visited the site but the guides knew little about their methods.

After three happy days in Lubaantun I departed, content in the knowledge that I had followed my intuition to the best of my ability and had learnt along the way to release any dependency on the result. Ultimately, we may never know the deeper purpose behind many of our life experiences and as I travel around the world I know a 'chance' encounter in an airport is as important as any pre-arranged meeting.

All that is asked of us is that we value every moment for what it is now and move beyond the need to analyse, compare or project our fantasies into the future. This does not preclude the need for planning for it is true to say that 'God *helps those who help themselves*'. But once we have prepared the scene as far as we can, it is then prudent to stand back and allow the *waters of time* to run their course.

Another facet of the story is to show that the intuition will entice us onto a path by using *bait* which is specific to our personality. So, in my case, this included *work, curiosity* and *a sense of purpose*. However, it is not uncommon to find that, once on the path, the impetus surrounding the original goal becomes diminished by events and a new attraction appears which leads us in a totally new direction.

When we elect to merge our will with the Will of our Creator and release our emotional attachment to future plans, we are given the opportunity to witness many miracles, contribute in a meaningful way and meet some extraordinary people. Looking back over the events in your life, you may notice times when you were enticed to move by an attracting force only to recognise in retrospect that the true reason for the gesture only became apparent when the journey was in progress.

Examples:

1   You attend a seminar on a subject which holds great interest for you, only to find that it is the person whom you sit next to at lunch who has the next clue for your journey.

2   You fall madly in love with someone who lives in another country and decide to move home to be with them. Nine months into the relationship, the love fades but by now you have enrolled in a college course which was not available in your own country and which on completion will lead to an exciting career change.

**Remember: Love is one of the most powerful
enticements for transformation.**

It is always easier for an observer to see the wider picture of our life whilst we remain obsessed with the initial goal. The intuition provides us with such an overview but requires us to act from a clear mind and open heart in response to **whatever** may emerge.

When the heart weeps for what it has lost,
the spirit laughs for what it has found.
Sufi aphorism

Seeds and symbols

If our plans are going to change and our expectations fail to materialise, why should we ever start the journey? If there are no guarantees, then why take the risk?

These are questions which are extremely valid and yet over thousands of years people have collected together their belongings and set out into unknown territory. Often the move was prompted by persecution or starvation but there are many stories of individuals and families leaving behind security, whether physical or mental, and trusting in their inner wisdom to follow a vision or, more poetically, *a travelling star.*

This is a separate issue from merely plucking a desire from the air in order to meet one's personal needs and then setting one's course to achieve it. When we follow *our* star there is a feeling that no other choice is available – whatever the consequences. It is not a selfish gesture but shows that now we are ready to listen and put our total trust in our inner voice.

I remember visiting a traditional Hawaiian village which had been reconstructed for tourists and formed the impression from its appearance that, during its heyday, the people lacked for nothing. There was ample food from the sea and the land, the houses were well-built, water was plentiful and yet, as I looked towards the horizon, I speculated on what had lured the young men to build their boats and leave this Utopia to seek other lands. In present day terms, there was no global media to transmit pictures of faraway places and I imagine that passing visitors would have been a rare event in the lives of these Pacific Islanders.

Did someone receive a vision in a dream or did the idyllic surroundings become routine and uninspiring? Probably we will never know; but inherent in the mind of every human being is the seat of curiosity and fascination nurtured by the signs, seeds and messages delivered by the intuition.

One reliable form of transmitting this information is through the use of *symbols* which are known to act mainly through the right brain, inducing abstract thought into consciousness. This impulse then passes across the corpus callosum (the link between the hemispheres) and into the left brain where concrete thought manifests.

Whatever the symbol, whether an image or a word, it stimulates our mind to produce a memory of something familiar as well as guide us to a place beyond reason and immediate meaning. As Jung says: *'Every symbol both reveals and conceals'*. In this way, our consciousness is seduced to reach beyond its normal parameters providing us with as many questions as there are answers.

A wonderful example of this phenomena is the *crop circles* which over the last 12 years have appeared around the world but especially in the fields of Southern England. Initially they took the form of simple circles and straight lines which were easily susceptible to claims of fraud or to scientific reasoning. However, the complexity of the formations over the past few years would defy any prankster and the search is still on for the identity of the *designer* of these organic masterpieces.

We know that there is a correlation between the thoughts of individuals on this earth plane and the development of a 'circle', and many of the designs contain symbols relevant to various religions and cultures around the world. But they offer much more as reflected in the sacred geometry of the formations, which is so specific and totally in accordance with many of the great ancient symbols of past civilisations such as the pyramids of Egypt.

It is now becoming clear that symbols, shapes and patterns have an amazing effect on our subconscious especially those which are known as the *Platonic* solids which include the:

- Hexahedron (the cube) – 6 faces
- Tetrahedron (the pyramid) – 4 faces
- Octahedron – 8 faces
- Dodecahedron – 12 faces
- Icosahedron – 20 faces

Such solids are the building blocks for many of the Sacred formations found throughout the world especially in sites of initiation; these include the Mayan temples of Central America, the temples and pyramids of Egypt, the shrines and ancient cities of Peru, the temples of Greece and the stone circles of Britain. It is believed that, in the past, it was necessary only to look upon these edifices in order to experience a change in brain-wave patterns and hence in consciousness.

In a similar way, mandalas, intricate mosaics and mazes have been found within Sacred Sites and appear to have been used to alter the brain state of the individual to one which was more receptive to higher wisdom and the forces of healing. The magnificent Cathedral at Chartres in France, was obviously designed by an architect who understood the mystical nature of the human mind, for here we find beautiful stained-glass windows in exquisite, healing colours and a labyrinth of initiation, intricately depicted on the church's floor.

Symbolism is a powerful means of expanding consciousness and its emergence at this time in our spiritual evolution is acting as a key to open the portals of our awareness which have been sealed for so long.

The crop circles and other recent phenomena are stimulating our curiosity and encouraging us to connect consciously with the *One Mind* through the qualities of hope, delight and compassion.

Visual imagery with colours and symbols

We can use any of the Platonic shapes as a focus for meditation and in the following exercise will work with the first three and include the eternal symbol of life, the wheel or sphere. The four images chosen are known to balance the four lowest chakras (the base, sacral, solar plexus and heart) although it is important during the imagery to lay aside any preconceived ideas concerning these energy centres and allow your intuition to guide you.

Find a place of comfort and sit or lie down. Close your eyes and take some deep breaths, relaxing your muscles and dissolving any unwanted thoughts from your mind. Enjoy the space of peace and quiet.

Coming towards you are different shapes and colours each with a brief outline of its meaning, although this is less relevant than the feelings and impressions which emerge from within you during the presentation of the symbols.

- So, after clearing the mind, see coming towards you a *red square, cube or hexahedron.*

  Watch as it moves and turns in front of you.

  It represents *structure, form, security and the element of earth.*

  Allow your own impressions to develop and store them in your memory.

- As the square/cube retreats and disappears, clear the mind and see coming towards you an *orange triangle, pyramid or tetrahedron.*

  This represents *harmony* and *equilibrium* and *the element of water.*

Allow yourself to view it from all perspectives and enjoy the experience.

Making a mental note of your impressions, watch as the triangle/pyramid fades.

- Clearing the mind, see coming towards you a *yellow diamond or octahedron* which represents *expansion, 'as above, so below', polarity and the element of air.*

Observe as it moves and dances in front of your eyes. Allowing impressions to develop, store these in your memory and watch as the image fades.

- Clearing the mind, see coming towards you a *green circle, ball or sphere* representing *the beginning and the end, life eternal, continuity and the element of fire.*

Watch as the shape turns in front of you enticing you to form your own impressions.

Storing any thoughts in your memory, let the image fade.

In your own time, bring your awareness back to the present moment and make a note of your findings in your journal.

These four shapes not only balance the lower four chakras but also expand consciousness and increase overall health. Your observations may correlate with the outlines provided above or you may find that the colours and symbols triggered a latent part of your mind to produce other images or thoughts which are relevant to your present situation. Practised regularly, this exercise and others which include colour and symbols, can greatly enhance your capacity to tune into your intuition.

10 True connection: merging the ego with the soul

What we call the beginning is often the end
And to make an end is to make a beginning.
The end is where we start from.

T.S. Eliot, *Four Quartets, 'Little Gidding',* **1942**

N ow at last we reach our final destination, the end of the journey and stand triumphant, looking back along the path we have just travelled. From our position we can see how it twists and turns, occasionally disappearing behind mountains or becoming lost in a thick forest before ascending steeply to its final conclusion.

It is easy to recognise the stages which were particularly challenging such as moving into the corridor or refusing to play power games and other occasions when we appeared to glide along the path powered only by Divine Inspiration. And we recall that when we set out on our journey the main purpose had been to find, trust and integrate our intuition and yet, along the way, we had received a bonus, for *we had found ourselves.*

We discovered a strength that was merely a flicker when we left home, a deep sense of inner peace untouched by daily life, an unconditional compassion for ourselves and others, a clarity of mind which rises above the emotions and logic and an irrefutable belief that we are co-creators of this beautiful Universe.

At one level, we have developed a keen insight into our soul direction and purpose and yet, we are not in possession of a map. But now we are willing to stand and wait, recognising that impatience and frustration are purely throw-backs to the need of the ego to control the outcome. The timing of events is very important to the Universe, even though time does not exist as a commodity on any other plane except our own.

Indeed, the sign of a fully trained initiate is to **know when the time is right** and then to **employ just enough force or energy to achieve the optimal result.** Without learning these skills so much valuable effort is wasted especially when we appreciate that there is a finite amount available and that other pleasures await us when we use this energy wisely.

As we stand and experience the vibration of our heart and mind resonating with the heart and mind of the Universe, we realise that the self identity which we worked so hard to establish, has lost its importance and, with apparent ease, the personality merges with the soul. In this state of *Oneness*, our soul rejoices as it reconnects to its Source and from this perspective we observe, with wry humour, that this sense of unity was always present within us but that it was necessary to experience separation before we could accept the totality.

From this place of inner knowing, we radiate warm rays of gratitude to all those who have advised and supported us on our pilgrimage and, appreciating that every end gives birth to a new beginning, we await the call from deep within our soul to embark upon a new venture, in the absolute belief that our Intuition will always be there to guide us.

Meditation to meet our intuition

Find a quiet and comfortable place to meditate and sit or lie down.

Take some deep breaths to relax your muscles and your mind.

See yourself in front of the opening to a cave. Become aware of the surroundings; for some there may be trees and mountains and for others the sea and sand. Become aware of the colours, smells, sounds and the sensation of the sun or wind on your face and body and the strength of the ground beneath your feet.

Now look into the cave entrance. You see a passageway stretching deep within the rock; it appears to be lit by a green luminous light of unknown origin, inviting you to walk into the cave. You move inside and travel further and further from the world outside and yet you feel safe and impelled to continue.

Suddenly, the passageway opens into a wide cavern; through a hole in the roof a beam of sunlight penetrates the darkness. This is a place of exceptional beauty and enchantment where the light appears to strike multi-coloured crystals embedded in the walls. Soft music is playing although, once again, there is no evidence as to its source.

Although you have no memory of entering this cave before, you have a distinct sense of comfort and familiarity which persuades you to ask aloud:

'May I meet the guardian of this beautiful temple deep within Mother Earth?'

Suddenly, into your line of vision, comes the image of an individual who represents your Intuition; the part of you which is wise and loving and who has supported you from the birth of your soul.

Observe the appearance of your Intuition. As you greet each other as eternal friends, know that the bond is one of unconditional love.

Enjoy the feeling of deep connection throughout your being and the peace, strength and joy this brings.

Your Intuition is willing to answer a question which is in your mind at this time:

Ask your question and receive the answer.

It is now time to leave the cavern but, before you go, your Intuition offers you a gift:

Receive the gift. You may wish to give something in return: *Give your gift.*

Make your farewells and start back along the passageway knowing that your Intuition will always be with you as a loyal, loving and wise friend.

As you step out into the daylight, know that you have been changed by the experience and treasure the precious gift you received.

When you are ready, allow your awareness to return to the present moment and slowly open your eyes. Make a note of your findings in your journal and choose to bring to mind the image of your Intuition whenever you seek clarity and compassion.

Epilogue

(From *'Indian to Indian'*, an editorial from the Saskatchewan Indian, copyright of the Onaway Trust).

'We are the people, each with his or her own road to walk, yet each leading to the same epicentre. From my road I see the centre from a different perspective than you, but we both see the centre. You cannot make me walk on your road so that I see as you do. You cannot block my way so I no longer walk down mine. But you can tell me what the view looks like from **your** perspective and I will tell you what I see from **mine**. And if you see me sitting in the ditch, please tell me to get up and walk on. If I see you turning away from the centre then I can try to point you the way back.

But if you choose to dance to a different drum, go down a different road entirely, then I can do nothing except wish you a safe journey. So it is with us. We share a continuity of existence on this land. We care for the future of those as yet unborn and we listen to those who have gone before. We are thousands of individuals, each unique, but all related. We are walking towards the same centre, in a circle without an end'.

Suggested reading

Alice Bailey, *Esoteric Psychology*, 1934
  From Intellect to Intuition, 1932
  A Treatise on White Magic, 1936; The Lucis Trust Ltd., London
Hal Stone and Sidra Winkelman, *Embracing Ourselves; the Voice Dialogue Manual*; Nataraj Publishing, 1989
Edward Bach, *The Twelve Healers*; The C.W. Daniel Co. Ltd., 1933
James Redfield, *The Celestine Prophecy*; Bantam Books, 1995
John Kabat Zin, *Wherever you go there you are* (Mindfulness Meditation); Hyperion, New York, 1994
Barbara Marciniak, *Earth*; Bear and Co., Santa Fe, 1994
Sams and Carson, *Medicine Cards*; Bear and Co., Santa Fe, 1988
Carl G. Jung, *Man and his Symbols*; Arkana, 1964

Index